BEST PRACTICES in
DEVELOPMENT

ULI AWARD WINNING PROJECTS

Theodore C. Thoerig

Urban Land Institute

BEST PRACTICES in
DEVELOPMENT

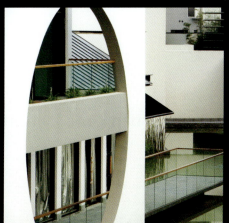

ULI AWARD WINNING PROJECTS

Project Staff

Rachelle L. Levitt
Executive Vice President
Information Group
Publisher

Dean Schwanke
Senior Vice President
Publications and Awards

David Takesuye
Director, Awards and Competitions
Project Director

Theodore C. Thoerig
Principal Author

Nancy H. Stewart
Director, Book Program
Managing Editor

Laura Glassman
Publications Professionals LLC
Manuscript Editor

Betsy VanBuskirk
Creative Director

Karrie Underwood
Digital Images Assistant

Craig Chapman
Director, Publishing Operations

Design and Composition

John Hall Design Group
Beverly, Massachusetts
www.johnhalldesign.com

Jennifer Mineo
Design Assistant

ULI–the Urban Land Institute
1025 Thomas Jefferson Street, N.W.
Suite 500 West
Washington, D.C. 20007-5201

Library of Congress Cataloging-in-Publication Data

Thoerig, Theodore, C.
  Best practices in development: ULI award winning projects 2008 / Theodore Thoerig.
     p. cm.
  1. Land use, Urban. I. Urban Land Institute. II. Title.
  HD1391.T56 2008
  333.77'150973-dc22

                                    2008029703

ISBN: 978-0-87420-110-9

10 9 8 7 6 5 4 3 2 1

Printed and bound in China.

About the Urban Land Institute

The mission of the Urban Land Institute is to provide leadership in the responsible use of land and in creating and sustaining thriving communities worldwide. ULI is committed to

- Bringing together leaders from across the fields of real estate and land use policy to exchange best practices and serve community needs;
- Fostering collaboration within and beyond ULI's membership through mentoring, dialogue, and problem solving;
- Exploring issues of urbanization, conservation, regeneration, land use, capital formation, and sustainable development;
- Advancing land use policies and design practices that respect the uniqueness of both built and natural environments;
- Sharing knowledge through education, applied research, publishing, and electronic media; and
- Sustaining a diverse global network of local practice and advisory efforts that address current and future challenges.

Established in 1936, the Institute today has more than 40,000 members worldwide, representing the entire spectrum of the land use and development disciplines. ULI relies heavily on the experience of its members. It is through member involvement and information resources that ULI has been able to set standards of excellence in development practice. The Institute has long been recognized as one of the world's most respected and widely quoted sources of objective information on urban planning, growth, and development

A guiding principle of the Urban Land Institute is that the achievement of excellence in land use practice should be recognized and rewarded. Since 1979, ULI has honored outstanding development projects in both the private and public sectors with the ULI Awards for Excellence program, which today is widely recognized as the development community's most prestigious awards program. ULI Awards for Excellence recognize the full development process of a project, not just its architecture or design—although these elements play an important role in the overall project. Each award is presented to the development project, with the developer accepting on behalf of the project.

Nominations are open to all, not just ULI members. Finalists and winners are chosen by juries of ULI full members chaired by trustees. Jury members represent many fields of real estate development expertise, including finance, land planning, development, public affairs, design, and other professional services. They also represent a broad geographic diversity.

ULI began the Awards for Excellence program in 1979 with the objective of recognizing truly superior development efforts. The criteria for the awards involve factors that go beyond good design, including leadership, contribution to the community, innovations, public/private partnership, environmental protection and enhancement, response to societal needs, and financial success. Winning projects represent the highest standards of achievement in the development industry, standards that ULI members hold worthy of attainment in their professional endeavors. All types of projects have been recognized for their excellence, including office, residential, recreational, urban/mixed use, industrial/office park, commercial/retail, new community, rehabilitation, public, and heritage projects, as well as programs and projects that do not fit into any of these product categories.

For the first three years of the program, only one Award for Excellence was granted each year. In 1982, ULI trustees authorized awards for two winners—one large-scale project and one small-scale project—to recognize excellence regardless of size. Starting in 1985, the awards program shifted emphasis to product categories, while also retaining the small- and large-scale designations. As the program matured, new categories were added to reflect changes in the development industry. In 2002, the last year in which winners were awarded by category, there were 18 categories and up to 11 possible awards.

The Special Award was established in 1986 to acknowledge up to two projects and/or programs that are socially desirable but do not necessarily meet the official awards guidelines governing financial viability, and exemplary projects that are not easily categorized. In 1989, the Heritage Award was introduced to acknowledge projects that have established an industry standard for excellence, and that have been completed for at least 25 years. As of 2008, only eight Heritage Awards have been granted.

When the awards program began, only projects located in the United States or Canada were considered. Beginning with the 1994 awards, ULI's board of trustees authorized the creation of an International Award for a project outside the United States and Canada. With the 2001 awards, the board eliminated this category, opening all categories to all projects, regardless of location.

In 2003, ULI eliminated all category designations, with the exception of the Heritage Award, and did more to recognize the excellence of all the finalist projects in the awards process, not just the award winners. In 2004, ULI inaugurated the ULI Awards for Excellence: Europe, adopting the same criteria and a similar selection process, and juried by Europe-based ULI members. And in 2005, the Awards for Excellence program continued to evolve with the introduction of the ULI Awards for Excellence: Asia Pacific.

Also new in 2005 was the introduction of the ULI Global Awards for Excellence. A select jury of international members, charged with choosing up to five Global Award winners from among that year's 20 award-winning projects, announced three global winners in 2005. In each year since, five projects have won Global awards.

Because each year's Global Award winners are not announced in time for publication in that year's book, the previous year's winners are recognized in this annual publication (see page 210).

The 2009 "Call for Entries" for the Americas, Europe, and Asia Pacific competitions is now available on the ULI Awards Web page (www.awards.uli.org).

THE ULI AWARDS FOR EXCELLENCE PROGRAM

JUDGING CRITERIA

1. Although architectural excellence is certainly a factor, the ULI Awards for Excellence is not a "beauty contest."

2. The project or program must be substantially completed. If the project is phased, the first phase must be completed and operationally stable.

3. No specific age or time constraints apply, except for the Heritage Award (which recognizes projects and/or programs that have been completed for at least 25 years).

4. The project must be financially viable, which means it must be in stable operation and financially successful. An applicant must be able to document the prudent use of financial resources to justify the achievement of a financial return. Programs and projects developed by nonprofit or public agencies are necessarily exempt from the financial viability requirement.

5. The project must demonstrate relevance to the contemporary and future needs of the community in which it is located. The community reaction to the project also is taken into consideration.

6. The project must stand out from others in its category.

7. The project must be an exemplary representative of good development and a model for similar projects worldwide.

SELECTION PROCESS

1. Applications are solicited via a "Call for Entries," available as a downloadable document on the ULI Web site's Awards page (www.awards.uli.org) on November 1.

2. Developers and/or other members of the development team submit completed applications to ULI by a given date in February. Each completed entry must contain the developer's name and signature.

3. The three Awards for Excellence juries—the Americas, Europe, and Asia Pacific—separately convene to review submissions and choose finalists.

4. Teams of two or three jury members visit each finalist project.

5. When all site visits have been completed, the respective juries reconvene to evaluate the finalist projects and choose award winners—up to ten in the Americas, five in Europe, and five in Asia Pacific. In the Americas, the jury may also choose one Heritage Award winner.

The Americas awards are announced and officially honored at an awards ceremony at ULI's annual Spring Council Forum. The Europe and Asia Pacific awards are announced at their respective spring or summer conferences. The Global awards are announced and officially honored at ULI's Fall Meeting.

CONTENTS

Commercial

Mixed Use

Residential/Planned Community

Civic

PHOTOGRAPHS BY JAMES STEINKAMP (T); ANTON GRASSL (TM); TIBO.ORG (BM); JEFF GOLDBERG, ESTO PHOTOGRAPHICS (B)

COMMERCIAL

PHOTOGRAPHS BY AVEQ FOTOGRAFIE (1L); DAVID PAPAZIAN (1LC); H.G. ESCH (1RC); A. PODBIELSKA (1R)

Adidas Village

PORTLAND, OREGON

The 11-acre (4.5-ha) Adidas Village, a redevelopment of the Bess Kaiser Hospital complex in North Portland, marks the consolidation of the global corporation's dispersed, suburban offices into a central urban campus. Through a clever mix of adaptive use and new construction, the corporate village transcends a myriad of site constraints while transforming a formerly moribund project area into a community asset. The new headquarters for Adidas's North American operations consists of 360,000 square feet (33,445 m^2) of office and design space, a large fitness center, playing fields, a public park, a restaurant, and an 830-space underground parking garage.

After relocating its operations from New Jersey in 1993, Adidas spent five years in Beaverton, Oregon, an outer suburb of Portland characterized by chain restaurants and strip malls. Home to Adidas's chief competitor in the sportswear industry, the Beaverton location was a poor fit with the company's demographically young workforce, whose lives revolved around urban—rather than

JURY STATEMENT

Adidas's decision to relocate from its suburban headquarters to an urban campus, converging with Winkler Development's plans to develop a former hospital site, has brought 800 employees to North Portland, has returned to the community a neighborhood asset with playing fields and other recreational amenities, and has reaffirmed a new corporate image and branding stewardship.

DEVELOPMENT TEAM

Owner
adidas America, Inc.
Portland, Oregon
www.adidas-group.com

Developer
Winkler Development Corporation
Portland, Oregon

Design Architect
BOORA Architects
Portland, Oregon
www.boora.com

Interior Architect
LRS Architects
Portland, Oregon
www.lrsarchitects.com

Landscape Architect
Lango Hansen Landscape Architects
Portland, Oregon
www.langohansen.com

suburban—activities. In 1998, seeking to consolidate its 11 Beaverton offices and tap into the creative workforce of downtown Portland, Adidas decided to build an urban headquarters modeled on a European-style village.

When the Bess Kaiser Hospital closed in 1996, Kaiser Permanente, the owner, decided to sell the complex rather than spend millions in seismic upgrades and maintenance repairs. Winkler Development purchased the site for $20 million with designs to construct housing, an office building, a daycare center, and an arts facility on the property, which straddled a four-lane highway. Two years later, the local Portland developer changed course, agreeing to a long-term, build-to-suit lease with Adidas, and then again in 2000, Winkler sold the site and buildings outright to the sports apparel manufacturer—an ownership structure unique within Adidas's global operations. Acquiring the site was a function of the build-to-suit amenities requested by Adidas, such as playing fields and a large fitness center, but it was also a reflection of the company's commitment to the community.

Built in 1959, the Bess Kaiser Hospital's drab, disjointed buildings—unused for over a decade—did little to inspire hope in the transformation envisioned by the development team. Inside the former hospital, the floor plates were heavily partitioned, and the sealed structure had little connection with the outside environment. The building also needed a $5 million seismic upgrade—more than it would cost to demolish the structures and start anew.

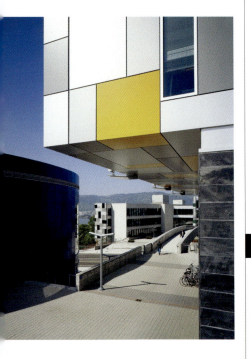

Led by BOORA Architects, the design team was convinced its vision for the site would overcome these challenges. By clearing all nonstructural walls, daylight now fills the interior spaces, drastically improving the indoor environment. To minimize the physical disconnect created by the Greeley Avenue truck route, which bisects the site, the architects visually extended the wedge-shaped entry plaza at the center of the existing complex across the busy thoroughfare. This move created a large, central open space, providing a tangible connection that unites the site and draws all traffic—employees, neighbors, and visitors—into the open-air plaza. Using the steeply sloping site to its advantage, the design team buried the 830-space parking garage beneath the elevated eastern side, placing the playing fields and new buildings on top. Doing so had the added benefit of reducing the impervious surface area and eliminating employee parking on neighborhood streets.

In contrast to most corporate headquarters, which tend to be isolated compounds adrift in a sea of parking and are often bunkered from their surroundings by berms and security checkpoints, Adidas Village is well integrated into the adjacent residential community. To create an appropriate interface with Adidas's neighbors, BOORA Architects clustered the new four-story buildings along the Greeley Avenue streetfront, while the playing fields and a public park buffer the surrounding one-story

SITE PLAN

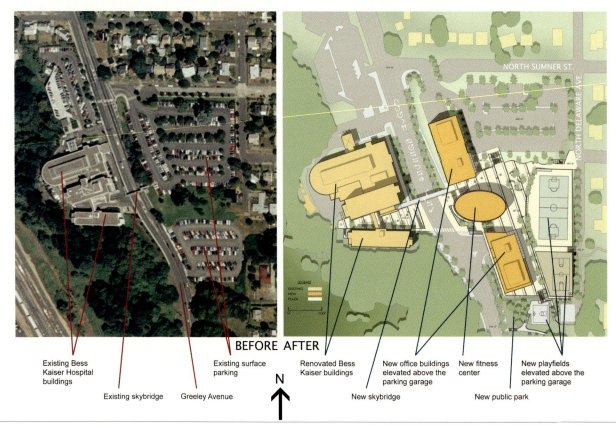

BEFORE   AFTER

Existing Bess Kaiser Hospital buildings

Existing skybridge   Greeley Avenue

Existing surface parking

N

Renovated Bess Kaiser buildings

New office buildings elevated above the parking garage

New skybridge

New fitness center

New public park

New playfields elevated above the parking garage

homes. The recreational fields are open to the public, and the skybridge provides safe passage for neighbors to access the mass transit across the busy thoroughfare.

The existing structures were not the only elements recycled at the Bess Kaiser site; the development team actively reused building materials or diverted them from the landfill. Almost all doors, lights, and sconces were reused; all discarded metal or concrete was recycled; and extra toilets, cabinetry, and counters were routed to Portland's Rebuilding Center, providing affordable construction materials for homeowners, artists, and contractors in the area.

The clean, modern aesthetic of the project broadcasts the corporate image of Adidas without relying on overt signage and logos. The design team clad the new structures and portions of the old buildings with an aluminum panel system, using five colors—red, yellow, green, blue, and black. Besides visually unifying the reused and newly constructed buildings, the colors mirror those used in the Olympic rings, reinforcing the company's commitment to global sport.

The new in-town locale—accessible by light rail, bus service, and dedicated bike lanes—also contributes to a reduced environmental footprint. Building retrofits reduced energy demand; high-performance windows have improved the efficiency of the existing structures by 40 percent. Designed before the U.S. Green Building Council's LEED (Leadership in Energy and Environmental Design) process was launched, Adidas Village obtained certification from Earth Advantage, the Pacific Northwest's premier green building program.

Completed for $63 million—$3 million under budget—Adidas Village has resurrected a decaying site, establishing a vibrant nexus of activity in its place. Providing ample room for Adidas's North American operations without overwhelming the surrounding residential neighborhood, the project has become an integral part of burgeoning North Portland.

PROJECT DATA

Website
www.adidas-group.com

Site Area
11 ac (4.5 ha)

Facilities
360,000 sf (33,445 m²) office
   completed
680,000 sf (63,174 m²) office at
   buildout

Land Uses
office, park/open space, parking

Start/Completion Dates
January 1999–January 2003

Elements at Kowloon Station

HONG KONG, CHINA

Elements at Kowloon Station is an 82,750-square-meter (890,714-sf) retail complex at the heart of Union Square, the largest mixed-use development in Hong Kong. The high-end shopping center brings to the vast minicity, built on reclaimed land, retail and nightlife opportunities for residents, businesspersons, and visitors. Situated near the southern coast of Kowloon,

DEVELOPMENT TEAM

Owner/Developer
MTR Corporation Limited
Hong Kong, China
http://www.mtr.com.hk/

Design Architect
Benoy
London, United Kingdom
www.benoy.com

Architect of Record
Aedas
London, United Kingdom
www.aedas.com

JURY STATEMENT

Elements at Kowloon Station, in the open center of the Union Square megablock, is the final, integrating piece of the plan to transform reclaimed land at Kowloon Bay into a new commercial center for Hong Kong. The interior shopping mall and outdoor public spaces link Union Square's 21 towers—including the 118-story ICC tower, Hong Kong's tallest—while connecting the development to the city's subway system.

Elements at Kowloon was developed around two Mass Transit Railway (MTR) stations, providing vital links to Hong Kong and Lantau islands.

Elements at Kowloon is the capstone for Union Square, a megadevelopment that was first conceived in the early 1990s as an integral component of a larger master plan for the area around Kowloon Station. The vision for the plan was simple: concentrate strategic commercial centers and communities along the subway that would achieve symbiotic success, supporting and sustaining each other in an economically viable manner. The first component built was Union Square, a mixed-use complex that includes 21 towers between 35 and 69 stories—housing more than 5,800 residential units, 2,230 hotel rooms, and approximately 232,258 square meters (2.5 million sf) of office space—arranged on the perimeter of the 13.5-hectare (33.5-ac) site. The colossal project includes the International Commerce Center (ICC) tower—now half built and slated for completion in 2010—that is expected to become Hong Kong's tallest building. Completed in October 2007, Elements at Kowloon Station sits at the tapered base of the ICC tower and opens onto the complex's 6.5-hectare (16.1-ac) central park.

Early in the planning stage, it became clear that a key design challenge would be addressing differences in scale: the surrounding project—rising to heights of 484 meters (1,588 ft)—dwarfs the two-story Elements at Kowloon. To reconcile this difference, the developer allocated a significant portion

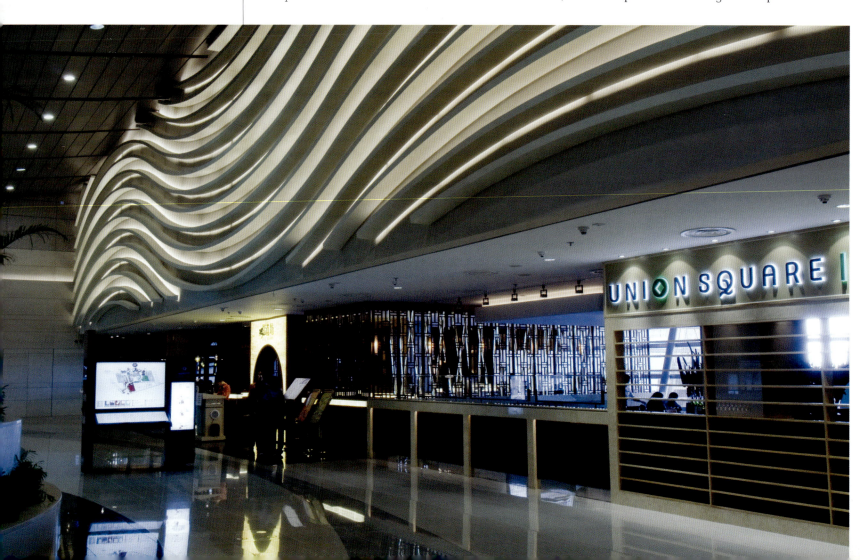

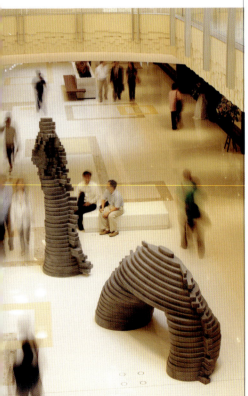

of the retail complex's restaurants and cafés to the civic square, forming an iconic outdoor hub of activity with the majestic towers as a backdrop. Also, the shopping center was designed to integrate seamlessly with the adjoining park and terraced gardens, creating a central, expansive leisure area that fills the site's interior.

The two-story retail complex is perforated by 3,716 square meters (40,000 sf) of skylights, reducing the need to rely on artificial lighting. Other sustainable design elements include a green roof; the use of double-glazed, low-emissivity glass in skylights and transparent walls; custom-designed elliptical entrances to prevent cool air from escaping the indoor environment; and energy-saving dual-speed escalators. Also, the project's access to two stations on Hong Kong's extensive MTR system encourages visitors and residents to use public transportation.

Managed by the development arm of MTR Corporation Limited, a private company that operates Hong Kong's public subway and light-rail system, the retail center links two separate mass-transit zones at either end of the complex, 250 meters (820 feet) apart, leading to a horizontal design. Such a linear layout is rare in the dense, vertical city of Hong Kong, and the design team, by necessity, created a stimulating and diverse retail design to animate the shopping experience.

The design concept, created by the architecture firm Benoy, originated from historic Chinese examples in which retail districts were segregated by the goods offered—for instance, a city would have a shoe street, a wedding street, or a market street. Adopting this notion of shopping quarters, the retail mix was divided into broad zones of entertainment, home, luxury, fashion, and food.

After each of the districts had been established in the overall retail plan, the design team explored the idea of using distinct themes to brand the zones, instilling each area with its own identity. Responding to the absence of nature in Hong Kong, the design team seized upon the feng shui–inspired five elements: earth, wood, metal, water, and fire. For instance, the entertainment district became the fire zone, with red and orange hues highlighting the space, and a large red sculptural wall became a dramatic addition to the large central area. The differentiated retail zones shape a sequence of distinct spaces that orient the shopper within the larger complex.

PROJECT DATA

Website
www.elementshk.com

Site Area
13.5 ha (33.5 ac)

Facilities
82,750 m² (890,714 sf) retail

Land Uses
retail, restaurant, entertainment, parks/open space, parking

Start/Completion Dates
August 2005–October 2007

SITE PLAN

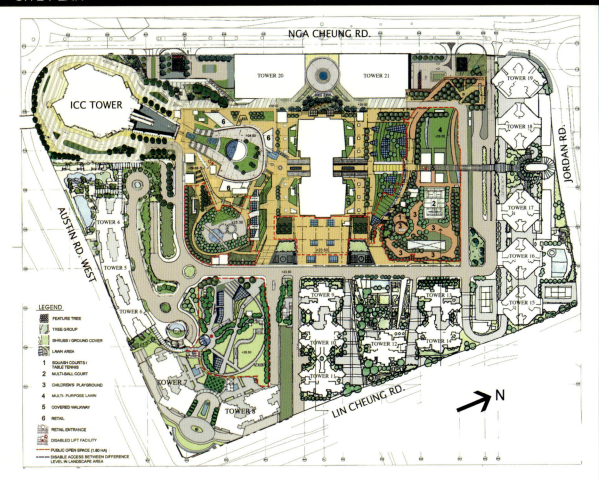

LEGEND

FEATURE TREE
TREE GROUP
SHRUBS / GROUND COVER
LAWN AREA
1 SQUASH COURTS / TABLE TENNIS
2 MULTI-BALL COURT
3 CHILDREN'S PLAYGROUND
4 MULTI-PURPOSE LAWN
5 COVERED WALKWAY
6 RETAIL
   RETAIL ENTRANCE
   DISABLED LIFT FACILITY
   PUBLIC OPEN SPACE (1.80 HA)
   DISABLE ACCESS BETWEEN DIFFERENCE LEVEL IN LANDSCAPE AREA

Kraanspoor

AMSTERDAM, THE NETHERLANDS

The historic derrick track where the Kraanspoor now stands was slated for demolition in 1997 when architect Trude Hooykaas was cycling through the NDSM shipyard of Amsterdam, in search of new studio space for her expanding architecture firm. Where most would overlook the nondescript, concrete mass among the other shipyard relics, Hooykaas envisioned a modern, sustainable office building for her practice. In 2007, the three-story, 12,500-square-meter (134,549-sf) Kraanspoor ("craneway" in Dutch) was completed, the first new development in the emerging district of Amsterdam North.

DEVELOPMENT TEAM

Owner/Developer
ING Real Estate Development
The Hague, The Netherlands
www.ingrealestate.com

Design Architect
OTH Ontwerpgroep Trude Hooykaas bv
Amsterdam, The Netherlands
www.oth.nl

JURY STATEMENT

By constructing a new three-story office building atop a functionally obsolete harbor structure on Amsterdam's IJ River, the developer minimized the environmental impact by retaining the mass of concrete, thus not disturbing the riverbed with new foundations, while also preserving a relic of the harbor's industrial past. The energy-efficient office space includes a double-skin façade and takes advantage of its waterfront location with a hydrothermal heating and cooling system.

Built in 1952, the derrick track once supported the shipbuilding cranes of the former NDSM shipyard in Amsterdam, on the north side of the River IJ. Because of the realignment of the Dutch shipbuilding industry, the once prosperous and bustling shipyard had been virtually abandoned for the past two decades. In recent years, however, the industrial buildings of the expansive shipbuilding yard gradually have been converted to studios for artisans and designers. Seeking to take advantage of affordable, underused space outside the high-rent central city of Amsterdam, an independent organization calling itself Kinetisch Noord approached the local council with a plan to redevelop the former shipyard into an expansive work space for art, design, and cultural activities. Kraanspoor stands as the first project completed in this creative hub of Amsterdam North.

The craneway itself is 270 meters (886 ft) long and 8.7 meters (28.5 ft) wide, approximately the length and width of a block-long street. It runs alongside the riverbank of the River IJ and rests on a pier foundation driven into the riverbed. The new, three-story, steel-frame office building atop the craneway occupies roughly the same footprint, accentuating the slender length of the industrial monument. The new edifice is lifted three meters (9.8 ft) above the craneway by thin steel columns, creating the impression that it floats above its foundation. The juxtaposition between the transparent modern aesthetic of the Kraanspoor and its hulking, concrete base further contributes to this lightness.

PROJECT DATA

Website
www.kraanspoor.nl

Site Area
1.3 ha (3.1 ac)

Facilities
12,500 m² (134,549 sf) office
175 parking spaces

Land Uses
office, parking

Start/Completion Dates
April 2006–November 2007

Fashioning a building foundation from the existing derrick track—which was designed to support heavy-duty, industrial cranes—without exceeding the load the structure was originally designed to withstand created a unique design challenge. The architect designed a sleek, simple structure with lightweight steel framing and flooring, which minimized the total load and allowed the construction to reach three floors. The design team even took advantage of the asymmetrical load-bearing features of the original craneway: because the derrick track was designed to support the cranes working over the river, the architect was able to incorporate a cantilevered overhang on the water-side of the building without compromising structural integrity.

The Kraanspoor incorporates a number of sustainable features in addition to the reuse of the historic craneway. The glass building's trademark feature is its transparent, double-skin façade: the outer curtain wall consists of solar-glazed, moveable louvers; the inner façade is made up of hinged, floor-to-ceiling windows. The air cavity between the two planes acts as a thermal buffer, insulating the offices from extreme heat or cold, and the motorized louvers on the outer wall allow natural ventilation of the interior space during mild seasons.

The internal climate of the Kraanspoor is regulated by a hydrothermal heat pump system that uses the relatively mild temperatures of the river as a heat sink. During the summer months, water from the river is pumped in to cool the building; in the winter, the relatively warm waters are used to pre-heat the central heating system. Also, a hollow floor design allows individual control over airflow, and a low-energy mechanical extraction system ventilates the building.

Given the waterfront locale, the craneway has always attracted nesting waterbirds. The development team built bird boxes below the structure to prevent disruption of the existing ecosystem, reinforcing the building's light and unassuming presence along the harbor.

The flexible design of the exterior and interior space extends the life cycle of the Kraanspoor beyond its current function as an office building. The interior has an open layout that can be easily reconfigured, and the removable top of the underfloor system permits easy access to electrical and mechanical systems.

Components of the original craneway have been incorporated into the building's new function. The four original stairwells remain as entrances to the building, modernized with panoramic elevators and new stairs. The two gangways alongside the concrete structure now serve as the fire escapes for the office development, and the basement of the derrick track has been converted into extensive archive and storage space.

Medinah Temple–Tree Studios

CHICAGO, ILLINOIS

Just one year before Albert Friedman of Friedman Properties purchased the Medinah Temple–Tree Studios complex, it appeared on the World Monuments Fund's list of 100 most-endangered sites. At the time, the cultural landmark was under threat from encroaching high-rise development, but a mix of innovative adaptive use and financing plans saved it from demolition. Today, Medinah Temple–Tree Studios has become a vibrant commercial complex with 165,000 square feet (15,329 m²) of home furnishing–themed retail space and 58,300 square feet (5,416 m²) of office/studio space geared toward artists and other creative professionals.

The former temple's dark interior has been radically transformed into a modern, airy, bright retail space, featuring a central atrium with glass elevators flanked by escalators while preserving such historic features as stained-glass windows and an ornate ceiling. The temple's four-level, 4,300-seat auditorium—which once hosted performers as diverse as the Chicago Symphony Orchestra and the Shrine Circus—has been converted to a Bloomingdale's Home store, the project's anchor.

Medinah Temple—built in 1912 as the Chicago headquarters for the Shriners organization—is considered one of the nation's finest examples of Islamic revival–style architecture. The adjacent Tree Studios, dating from 1894, with annexes added in 1912 and 1913, was designed as studios and housing for artists and artisans—the oldest artists colony in the United States. Notable studio residents have included author Edgar Rice Burroughs, sculptor Albin Polasek, and actor Peter Falk.

The two properties occupy an entire city block just west of the North Michigan Avenue shopping district. At the turn of the 21st century, both properties were owned by the Shriners organization, which sought to sell them to raise funds for its children's hospital. The block, like those surrounding it, was zoned for high-rise development, and a developer had offered more than $20 million for the properties, which it planned to demolish to create a site for a by-right 40-plus-story condominium building.

DEVELOPMENT TEAM

Owner/Developer
Friedman Properties, Ltd.
Chicago, Illinois
www.friedmanproperties.com

Public Partner
Chicago Department of Planning and
   Development
Chicago, Illinois
www.cityofchicago.org

Architect
Daniel P. Coffey & Associates, Ltd.
Chicago, Illinois
www.dpcaltd.com

JURY STATEMENT

Resisting the tide of surrounding high-rise development, Medinah Temple–Tree Studios stands as an oasis of immaculately restored landmark buildings around a central, landscaped courtyard. The historic Medinah Temple complex now houses a Bloomingdale's Home store, and the former Tree Studios carry on as retail spaces and studios for artists and artisans.

In 2000, the city created a tax increment financing (TIF) district for the exclusive benefit of the two properties on this block, a funding mechanism that enabled Friedman to purchase them for full market value in April 2001. Two months later, the Commission on Chicago Landmarks designated both properties a Chicago landmark, thus preventing their demolition and setting the stage for Friedman Properties, in conjunction with architect Daniel P. Coffey & Associates, to undertake an innovative adaptive use plan.

The $60 million renovation project—which made use of historic-preservation tax credits in addition to the TIF funding—began with the challenging transformation of the interior of the Medinah Temple into a four-story Bloomingdale's Home store. A new, all-steel structure was inserted within the building shell, the exterior walls, roof, and suspended plaster ceiling of which had been retained in place. The balconies and main floor of the auditorium were removed, and the basement was

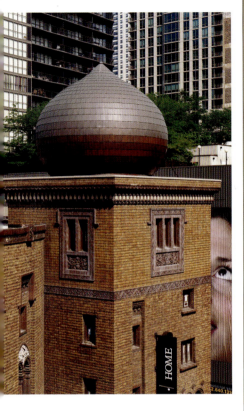

lowered four feet (1.2 m). An interior atrium capped by the auditorium's original plaster dome ceiling was created. The temple's long-lost, twin copper onion domes were re-created, and the store opened in early 2003.

Next, the original Tree Studios building and its annexes were meticulously restored and transformed into office/studio space and upscale shops. A landscaped interior courtyard provides a welcome oasis from the high rises on adjacent blocks. Completed in 2005, the restored Tree Studios is listed on the National Park Service's Register of Historic Places.

"The Medinah Temple–Tree Studios redevelopment was one of the most challenging projects undertaken in our company's 35-year history of adaptive use of historic properties," comments Albert M. Friedman, president of Friedman Properties. "In the face of a changing development environment where bigger is better, Medinah Temple–Tree Studios serves as a model of the collective creativity and resourcefulness that comes from a public/private partnership not only to save important historic buildings, but also to save the history and the soul of our city."

SITE PLAN

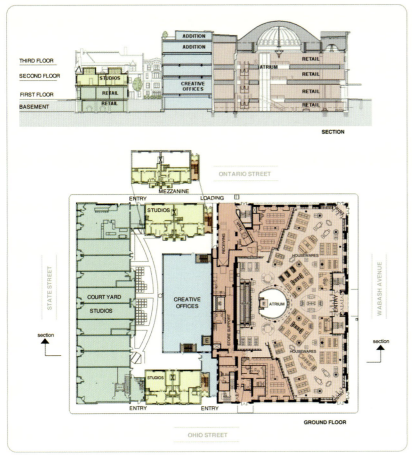

PROJECT DATA

Website
www.friedmanproperties.com/
  developments

Site Area
1 city block

Facilities
58,300 sf (5,416 m²) office
165,000 sf (15,329 m²) retail

Land Uses
retail, office

Start/Completion Dates
August 2001 (for phase1); 2003–2005
  (for phase 2)

Meydan Shopping Square

ISTANBUL, TURKEY

Boasting one of the largest geothermal cooling and heating systems in all of Europe, Meydan Shopping Square, opened in August 2007 by METRO Group Asset Management GmbH & Co., is a 70,000-square-meter (753,474-sf) modern marketplace in the emerging Umraniye district of Istanbul, Turkey. Designed by Foreign Office Architects (FOA) of London, the 50-store shopping square is covered by 30,000 square meters (322,917 sf) of natural roof meadows, vastly reducing stormwater runoff—a chronic problem with traditional shopping centers—and creating a large park system in the expanding Turkish megacity.

DEVELOPMENT TEAM

Owner/Developer
METRO Group Asset Management
  GmbH & Co.
Dusseldorf, Germany
www.metro-mam.de

Design Architect
Foreign Office Architects
London, United Kingdom
www.f-o-a.net

JURY STATEMENT

Capped by three hectares (7.4 ac) of undulating green roofs, the Meydan Shopping Square, a 70,000-square-meter (753,473-sf) shopping complex, has become a new center for Istanbul's emerging Umraniye district. Underground parking and Europe's most extensive geothermal heating and cooling system freed the surface of the 13-hectare (32-ac) site for meadows, lawns, and public plazas.

In 1950, Istanbul had a million inhabitants; today, it has 11 times that number. Umraniye, on the Asian side of the ancient city, is one of the fastest-growing districts in the sprawling metropolis. Just a few decades ago, it was an overlooked village on the road to the Sea of Marmara, whereas now, its population exceeds that of Washington, D.C. Unfortunately, this frantic growth has been unfocused, with scattershot development ignoring the public spaces and open landscapes necessary for a vibrant community—a void Meydan Shopping Square aspires to fill.

METRO Group Asset Management is part of the METRO Group—one of the largest retailers in the world. The company hosted a three-day design competition to build a prototype for a new shopping mall, inviting five architectural teams from across Europe to take part. The developer issued only two design mandates: the new building was to be an urban entertainment center for the Umraniye district and must not have anything in common with the inward-facing nature of traditional shopping malls.

A team of young architects from FOA—who, coincidentally, had no experience designing retail centers—won the competition with a design that paid particular attention to cultural and geographic context and emphasized the public sphere. The architectural firm began with the concept of the public square as a crossroad, where all routes intersect and congregations of people inevitably assemble.

Because of its unique geographic position, Istanbul has more geothermal energy potential than any other metropolitan area in the world. Sitting on a fault line between two continental plates may leave the city vulnerable to earthquakes, but it also generates copious amounts of heat: the temperature differences necessary for geothermal energy are five times greater here than normal. The system at Meydan Shopping Square saves 1.3 million kilowatt-hours of energy annually, is available at any time of the day or year, and has zero environmentally harmful emissions. Achieving a savings of 350 tons

of carbon dioxide annually, the developer expects the system to pay for itself in less than five years. According to the chief executive officer of METRO Group Asset Management, Professor Michael Cesarz, "It was an important goal—given the global increase in energy costs—to establish a forward-looking pilot project that exhibits the efficient use of regenerative forms of energy while satisfying the demand for economic viability."

The development team aspired to create a living, natural part of the city, which it accomplished by building Meydan Shopping Square under a greenfield, rather than paving over top of one. Referred to as the "fifth" façade, the three-hectare (7.4-ac) green roof follows the natural contours of the hilly Umraniye district, forming an undulating urban meadow atop the retail center. The expansive green roof not only offers residents and visitors recreational opportunities amid an expanding urban environment, but also insulates the shopping center from extreme temperatures, creating even more energy savings.

Situated on formerly vacant land between a highway junction and multiplying apartment blocks, Meydan Shopping Square contains more than 50 shops—including Turkey's first IKEA store—as well as a cinema and a number of restaurants and cafés. The stores, which are separated into thematic areas reminiscent of the bazaar streets along the Bosporus, are situated around the large public plaza that forms the center of the retail complex. Tiled with pervious, terra-cotta-colored bricks, the central square is connected to all levels of the complex by a series of ramps and staircases. A number of access points were established to accommodate visitors in cars, on foot, or riding bicycles from the surrounding neighborhood, which offers a clear divergence from traditional isolated shopping centers.

Providing ample, underground parking was a major part of FOA's design strategy. By eschewing the traditional surface parking lots associated with shopping malls, the design team liberated substantial amounts of the ground level for landscaping, the urban square, and additional leasable space.

Completed in the summer of 2007, Meydan Shopping Square has been a great success, attracting more than 55,000 daily visitors on the weekends. With the application of vegetation-covered roof levels and one of the largest geothermal systems in Europe, the retail center has become one of the most ecologically attractive shopping malls on the continent.

SITE PLAN

N

PROJECT DATA

Website
www.meydan.metro-mam.com

Site Area
13 ha (32 ac)

Facilities
70,000 m² (753,474 sf) retail
3,000 parking spaces

Land Uses
retail, restaurant, entertainment,
  open space, parking

Start/Completion Dates
March 2006–October 2007

Stadsfeestzaal

ANTWERP, BELGIUM

In December 2000, the Stadsfeestzaal, a historic festival hall in Antwerp, was ravaged by a fire that nearly destroyed the 100-year-old historic monument. Multi Development, in a joint investment with Bank of Ireland Private Banking, refurbished the 19th-century neoclassical building, restoring its luxurious character and converting it to a high-end shopping center. The four-level structure now consists of 20,500 square meters (220,660 sf) of retail space, 49 planned multifamily units, and 275 underground parking stalls and provides the missing link between two existing shopping districts.

DEVELOPMENT TEAM

Developer
Multi Development Belgium nv
Antwerp, Belgium
www.multi-development.com

Architect
T+T Design
Antwerp, Belgium

Owners
Multi Investment
Gouda, The Netherlands
www.multi-capital.com

Bank of Ireland
Dublin, Ireland
www.bankofireland.ie

JURY STATEMENT

The refurbishment of Antwerp's 100-year-old landmark festival hall, almost destroyed by fire in 2000, not only returns a cherished monument to the city center, but also adds a new locus of retail activity and connects two previously separated shopping districts. The Stadsfeestzaal exemplifies a successful public/private partnership and a restoration of a city's link to its history.

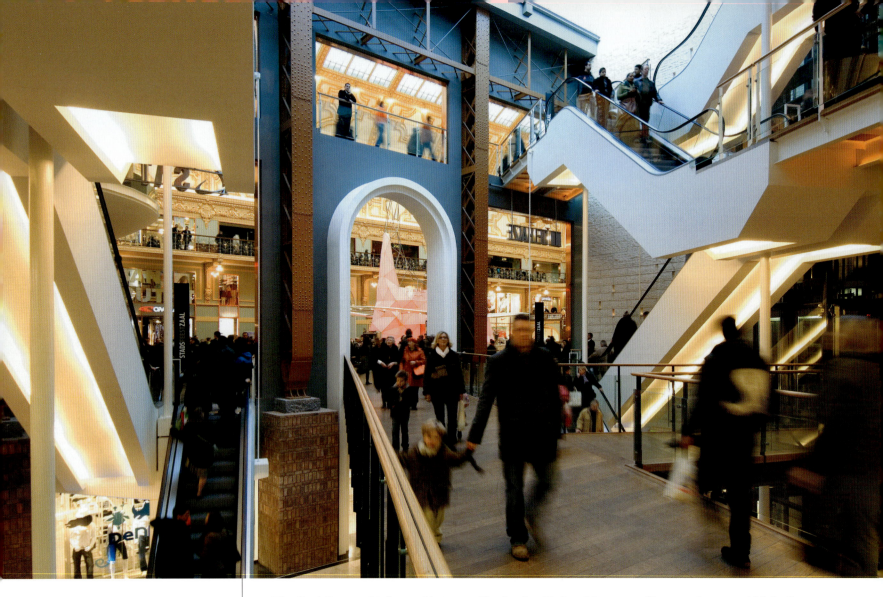

The Stadsfeestzaal is located between Hopland, with its wide range of luxury shops, and Meir, the popular retail street in Antwerp. The developer took advantage of the Stadsfeestzaal's unique position by constructing a ground-level passageway, completing the connection between the two shopping districts and capturing the foot traffic of each retail area's distinct clientele. The shops at the Stadsfeestzaal cater to a range of shoppers, allowing the retail complex to appeal to day-trippers and tourists as well as city residents.

Built in 1907, the Stadsfeestzaal ("City Festival Hall" in Flemish-speaking Antwerp) was once one of the city's most enduring attractions, serving as the natural venue for countless exhibitions and festivities. Since the 1980s, however, the Stadsfeestzaal had fallen into disuse, as public events moved to more spacious venues in the harbor city, such as the Antwerp Sports Palace. Although the structure badly needed refurbishment, the Antwerp municipal government did not have the public funds for the reconstruction. As a result, the city administration held an open competition in 1997 for private developers to redesign the space and restore the historic building.

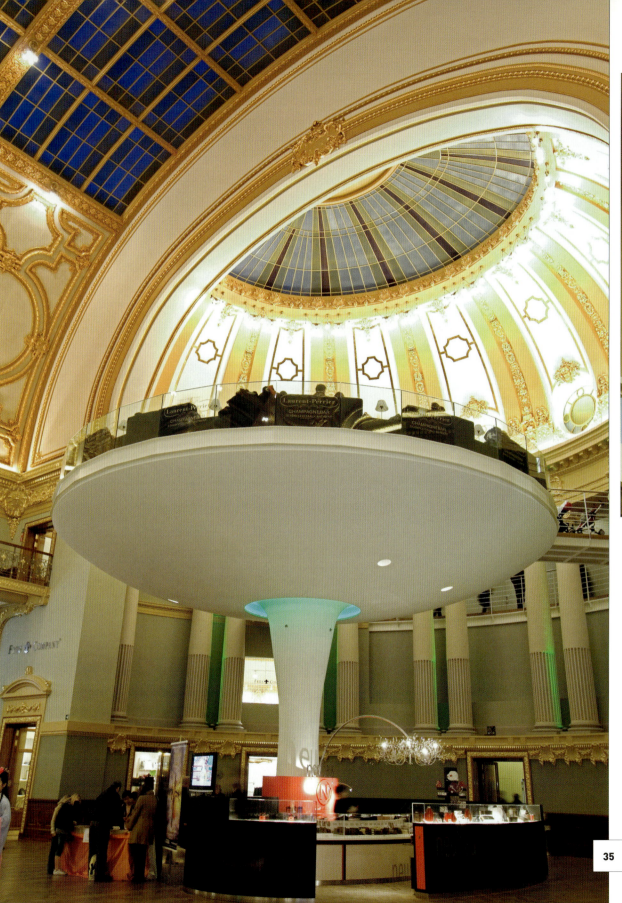

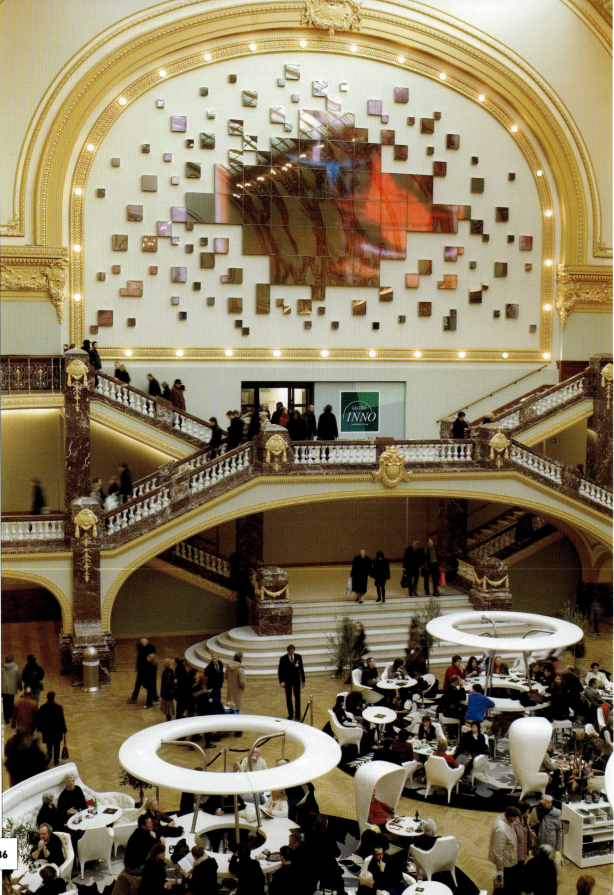

After being selected to redevelop the site, Multi Development entered into a long-term lease for the festival hall with an option to purchase the property. The properties surrounding the expansive hall—where most of the shops are concentrated—were sold outright to the retail developer.

Only a few months after Multi Development was selected to redevelop the Stadsfeestzaal, a fire ripped through the festival hall. The destructive blaze set the development process back significantly, but it also created new possibilities by opening an extra level for retail space.

After a three-year delay, construction and development resumed in 2004. The developer transformed the festival hall into a two-tiered shopping arcade, restoring the parquet flooring, extensive gold-leaf ornamentation, and enormous, arched glass roof. The original marble staircases were preserved, and the Stadsfeestzaal's trademark reliefs and friezes were meticulously restored. Along the Meir, the gilded archway entrance to the neoclassical structure has also been returned to prominence.

Although the Stadsfeestzaal is a historic structure, T+T Design, Multi Development's in-house designers, infused it with contemporary amenities. Two modern restaurants and bars—one of which is atop a champagne-saucer-shaped structure 7.5 meters (25 ft) high—are positioned at the center of the shopping arcade. Nevertheless, the presence of the modern additions was not overpowering: the design team was mindful to leave the traditional architecture visible from all vantage points.

Since it opened in October 2007, the Stadsfeestzaal has seen more than 25,000 people visit on an average day. The 40 shops are fully leased by national and international retailers, including many that are new to Belgium—the first Urban Outfitters in Europe is located at the retail complex. The project was a risky undertaking: many developers studied the site for redevelopment but were wary of the complexity of the refurbishment. Nonetheless, Multi Development's ten-year effort has been an economic success, returning a historic asset to the community and bolstering the city's most popular shopping district.

PROJECT DATA

Website
www.stadsfeestzaal.com

Site Area
0.8 ha (2.0 ac)

Facilities
20,146 m² (216,850 sf) retail
49 multifamily units (proposed)
275 parking spaces

Land Uses
retail, restaurant, residential,
  parking

Start/Completion Dates
November 2004–October 2007

Unilever House

LONDON, UNITED KINGDOM

Commissioned by its namesake corporation in 1932, the 24,121-square-meter (259,636-sf) Unilever House occupies a prominent site on the north bank of the Thames River. The redevelopment of the Grade II–listed office building achieves a balance between retaining the building's historic façade and providing an open-air, flexible work space necessary for the global corporation's day-to-day operations. Sustainable practices permeated all phases of the Unilever House rehabilitation, culminating in its Building Research Establishment Environmental Assessment Method (BREEAM) "Excellent" rating and an overall 25 percent carbon emission reduction.

In 2004, United Kingdom–based developer Stanhope began working with Unilever to consider options for its headquarters—including the possibility of relocating away from the historic Unilever

DEVELOPMENT TEAM

Owners/Developers
Stanhope PLC
London, United Kingdom
www.stanhopeplc.com

Sloane Blackfriars
London, United Kingdom
www.sloanecapital.com

Design Architect
Kohn Pedersen Fox Associates
London, United Kingdom
www.kpf.com

JURY STATEMENT

Unilever House, a Grade II–listed property originally commissioned in 1932, has undergone a refurbishment that restores its classical grandeur and commercial relevance in the city of London. The nine interior levels were removed and replaced with open, expansive spaces—built to BREEAM "Excellent" rating—and leased back to Unilever and other tenants.

House. However, the neoclassical building's assets—prime location, heritage, and recognition factor—ultimately convinced the company that it should remain in the structure. The project was financed on a sale and leaseback basis, where Sloane Capital acquired the property from Unilever, which then agreed to lease it back for 25 years.

Architect Kohn Pedersen Fox sought to preserve the iconic features of Unilever House while drastically reconfiguring the interior to accommodate a modern work space. The façade along the Victoria Embankment—the building's most celebrated feature—was painstakingly restored, with a renewed emphasis on its 16 Ionic columns and large, arched windows. The entrance to the building was returned to the Embankment façade, and the famous "Thames Room" interior was enhanced and extended as part of the grand entry hall.

Lying just within the structure's historic exterior is a nine-level, thoroughly modern office building. The office layout, which was once compartmentalized and disjointed, now flows naturally, facilitating interactions and chance encounters between employees. The reconfigured, open-plan floor plates surround the central, light-filled atrium; a series of irregular floors is suspended by high-strength steel tension rods from the atrium ceiling to create additional meeting spaces; and the three elevator wells were consolidated into a single, glass-walled elevator in the center of the atrium, drawing activity to the center of the building.

The main meeting areas and conference rooms are located on the top floor of Unilever House, with a landscaped rooftop garden above. The mechanical systems were removed from the top of the building—improving views, eliminating an eyesore, and expanding space for events.

Principles of sustainability were applied throughout the development process, with the development team aspiring to reverse the carbon footprint produced by the 76-year-old building. After the

decision was made to restore and rehabilitate the existing structure, an initial audit assessed the overall efficiency of the building and established benchmarks to measure future performance. A detailed schedule inventoried every building feature, and all materials that could be reused or recycled were identified and catalogued. These preliminary steps established a quantitative baseline against which all sustainable efforts could be evaluated.

From the outset, a key aspect of the project was to minimize waste generation during demolition and construction and to maximize opportunities for reuse and recycling. From the high-quality parquet flooring that was discovered under the carpeting to the lecture theater, which was carefully disassembled for future use by an off-site heritage center, approximately 87 percent of removed building materials were reused or recycled. The development team engaged local charities to donate any unwanted furniture, ensuring as little material as possible made its way to the landfill.

Stanhope and the construction manager, Bovis Lend Lease, helped establish the London construction consolidation center. The facility, a few miles outside the congested city center, allowed construction materials to be stored until a full truckload could be consolidated, thus eliminating unnecessary trips, improving reliability, and reducing greenhouse gas emissions.

Completed in 2007, Unilever House managed a carbon emissions reduction of 25 percent—far greater than the requirement of London building regulations that govern refurbished buildings and even those that regulate new construction. The project also achieved an "Excellent" BREEAM rating and was commended for a number of innovative design features—all while achieving a 22 percent profit on cost. What had been an underperforming asset has been transformed into grade-A space through sustainable design and meticulous rehabilitation.

PROJECT DATA

Website
www.buildingunilever.com

Site Area
0.4 ha (0.9 ac)

Facilities
22,840 m² (245,848 sf) office
  completed
24,121 m² (259,636 sf) office at
  buildout

Land Uses
office, parking

Start/Completion Dates
October 2004–July 2007

ADIA Headquarters

ABU DHABI, UNITED ARAB EMIRATES

Soaring over 185 meters (607 ft) in height, the Abu Dhabi Investment Authority (ADIA) Headquarters building consolidates—along Abu Dhabi's famed Corniche beachfront—its sovereign wealth fund operations. Completed in 2007, the sinuous, slender tower contains 65,600 square meters (706,112 sf) of Class A office space and is surrounded by vast greenery, complementing the heavily landscaped Corniche. The elegant 37-story structure also responds to its environment, featuring a double-skin "active" façade, mechanized louvers for climate control, and a computer-controlled lighting system to conserve energy.

An eight-kilometer (five-mi) curved promenade along Abu Dhabi's northwest coastline and one of the city's most enduring attractions, the Corniche is the lush greenway area that earned Abu Dhabi the title "Garden City of the Gulf." The project was part of a multibillion-dirham facelift of the Corniche. Despite its prominent location, the 8.5-hectare (21-ac) site was underused. Formerly home to a small, one-story police station surrounded by parking, the project area was also segregated from the historic city center.

The curvilinear, flowing shape of the ADIA building stands in stark contrast to angular, Western-style skyscrapers. Inspired by images of billowing sails of the *dhows* (traditional Arab sailboats) and shifting sand dunes, the massing is simple: a vertical plane folded three times to create two slender wings. Rising between the two towers is an atrium 150 meters (492 ft) high that incorporates social

DEVELOPMENT TEAM

Owner/Developer
Abu Dhabi Investment Authority
Abu Dhabi, United Arab Emirates
www.adia.ae

Architect
Kohn Pedersen Fox Associates
   (International) PA
London, United Kingdom
www.kpf.com

Landscape Architect
EDAW Ltd.
London, United Kingdom
www.edaw.com

PROJECT DATA

Website
www.adia.ae

Site Area
8.7 ha (21.5 ac)

Facilities
65,600 m² (706,112 sf) office
2,501 m² (26,921 sf) retail
760 parking spaces

Land Uses
office, retail, entertainment, parking

Start/Completion Dates
March 2002–February 2007

spaces and vistas of the sea. An auditorium and a reception space provide a large, formal gathering area in the lower ground floor of the building. The corporate headquarters is surrounded by extensive landscaping, serving as a gentle transition between the green space of the Corniche and the ever-expanding skyline of the city center.

The architecture of the ADIA building is a modern interpretation of regional traditions. The slim towers are suggestive of the adjacent mosque's slender minarets, while the wings of the structure open toward the sea and Mecca. Punctuating the atrium are a series of "sky gardens," or communal spaces, which continue the Islamic tradition of planted areas within buildings and act as an extension of the urban parkway of the Corniche.

The ADIA Headquarter's most prominent sustainable feature is a double-skin, transparent façade that regulates the building's indoor climate and permits generous daylighting of the offices. The "active" façade, one of the first built in the Middle East, comprises three layers: a low-emissivity-coated, double-glazed outer skin, a single glass internal skin, and a solar-controlled blind within the cavity. Linked to a building management system, the fabric blinds respond to the path of the sun, closing when the rays strike the building face and opening when it falls into shadow. The structure's folded shape creates slender floor plates, allowing sunlight to penetrate the inner reaches.

The project also incorporates a computer-controlled lighting system that manages each fixture according to its location and user requirements. To conserve energy, the control system includes a presence sensor that shuts off lights in areas where there is no activity.

The design of the ADIA Headquarters began almost ten years ago, when many Middle East developments were still judged by regional standards; ADIA, however, envisioned a global headquarters that would stand out on the international stage. Today, the Gulf States are recognized as key players in world finance, and the ADIA Headquarters has become a distinctive symbol not only of Abu Dhabi as an international city but also of the increasingly important role its investments play in the global market.

The ADIA Headquarters provides the organization with modern, high-class office space that was previously lacking in this area of Abu Dhabi. The building satisfies the client's growing need for three distinct types of office space: private offices, open-floor-plan areas, and cross-departmental meeting spaces.

PHOTOGRAPHS BY H.G. ESCH

Gateway Mall

QUEZON CITY, PHILIPPINES

Gateway Mall is a five-level shopping center at the heart of an established commercial hub in Quezon City, one of the municipalities that constitute metropolitan Manila. Served by two elevated mass-transit lines, the 95,000-square-meter (1.02 million-sf) retail center features 168 shops, 28 restaurants, a ten-screen cineplex, a hotel banquet facility, a supermarket, and 8,623 square meters (672,744 sf) of office space. The urban infill development stands as the landmark project of a massive 20-year redevelopment plan by Araneta Center, Inc. (ACI).

Araneta Center—one of the Philippines' largest retail and entertainment developments—was begun in the 1960s and has been gradually built out to its current 35-hectare (87-ac) dimensions. Situated at the crossroads of Manila's two busiest highways and served by two separate mass-transit lines, Araneta Center is a bustling multimodal interchange: an estimated 1 million people pass through the area every day. In recent years, ACI has begun an ambitious, PHP 55 billion (US$1.25 billion) master plan to transform the district into a more contemporary mixed-use destination. By focusing on the country's growth sectors—middle-income housing and office space for outsourced business opera-

DEVELOPMENT TEAM

Owner/Developer
Araneta Center, Inc.
Quezon City, Philippines
aranetacenter.net

Architect/Master Planner
RTKL Associates, Inc.
Los Angeles, California
www.rtkl.com

tions—and enhancing its retail and entertainment holdings, ACI hopes to position Araneta Center as the central business district of Quezon City. Gateway Mall represents the first step toward realizing this massive redevelopment effort.

The retail center was developed on a 1.6-hectare (four-ac) site divided into parcels of different shapes, sizes, and grades—all crisscrossed by congested roadways. The two mass-transit stops on each side of the project area serve the north-south MRT3 and the east-west LRT2 lines, generating a steady stream of pedestrians transferring between trains—a dangerous proposition on Quezon City's hectic streets, already whirring with cars, motorbikes, and bicycles. Furthermore, the site slopes considerably, presenting the developers with the challenge of connecting two transit stations on varying elevations.

The PHP 2.6 billion (US$60 million) retail center was financed with equity investments from ACI and traditional loans from the two largest banks in the country—Bank of the Philippine Islands and Metropolitan Bank and Trust Company. Designed by RTKL Associates, Gateway Mall features five levels of retail space centered around a 465-square-meter (5,005-sf) water garden—an interior oasis that presented an engineering challenge—showcasing waterfalls, rare plants, and an 18-meter (60-ft) palm tree and bringing the lush, green landscape indoors. The development team initially feared the oasis could reduce visibility of surrounding shops; however, the verdant atrium has been a success, offering a calming natural element amid a frenzied urban environment.

In addition to featuring elevated connections to two separate mass-transit stations, Gateway Mall is linked to the 40,000-square-meter (430,556-sf) Araneta Coliseum, the largest indoor stadium in the Philippines. The network of covered walkways and enhanced sidewalks throughout the retail complex allows a safer pedestrian experience and improves vehicular circulation. Linking the project to the busy transit system and the popular sports arena has the added benefit of increasing foot traffic at the retail destination.

Gateway Mall's domestic water and fire protection needs are served by a 750,000-liter (198,129-gal) underground cistern. The dedicated water supply eliminated the need to drill deep wells, preserving the integrity of the area's water table. The developer also constructed a state-of-the-art sewage treatment facility under an active roadway. The retail center incorporates a variety of energy conservation measures: large windows allow extensive natural illumination; high-performance insulated glass minimizes solar heat gain; and the project is cooled by an energy-efficient, computer-controlled air-conditioning system.

Gateway Mall has greatly improved the pedestrian experience and intermodal convenience in the large metropolitan district, providing a modern retail destination for the growing middle class. As the benchmark project of the Araneta Center Master Plan, the retail center has catalyzed surrounding development: already under construction are a 30-level skyscraper directly connected on four levels to Gateway Mall; an 8,000-unit, high-rise residential development; a 743-square-meter (8,000-sf) cyberpark; and a luxury, 415-room business hotel.

SITE PLAN

PROJECT DATA

Website
www.gatewaymall.com.ph

Site Area
1.6 ha (4.0 ac)

Facilities
8,623 m² (672,744 sf) office
86,837 m² (26,921 sf) retail

Land Uses
retail, office, restaurant,
  entertainment, parking

Start/Completion Dates
February 2003–May 2005

Hotel Wasserturm

HAMBURG, GERMANY

As the Industrial Revolution reached Germany in the mid-19th century, urban centers began building central waterworks. Usage increased and water towers followed to maintain water pressure throughout the system. Water towers symbolized progress, and as highly visible landmarks—frequently built on hilltops because they were gravity powered—they were often designed as architectural icons. The *wasserturm* (water tower) in the Sternschanzen Park, a kilometer (0.62 mi) northwest of Hamburg's city center, is a prime example. One of only three remaining in Hamburg, which once had 43, this water tower—an octagonal brick edifice 60 meters (197 ft) tall and 25 meters (82 ft) in diameter—was particularly handsome.

It was built in 1910—and was the largest in Europe in its day—on the site of a reservoir in the park. As electric pumps replaced gravity to maintain water pressure, water towers became redundant. After World War II, when its roof was partially destroyed by bombs, the water tower was returned briefly to

DEVELOPMENT TEAM

Developer
Patrizia Projektentwicklung GmbH
Augsburg, Germany
www.patrizia.ag

Initial Developer
Ernst Joachim Storr
Munich, Germany

Hotel Operator
Mövenpick Hotels & Resorts
Glattbrugg, Switzerland
www.movenpick-hotels.com

Architect
Architekturbüro Falk von Tettenborn
Munich, Germany
www.tettenborn.net

its function and finally decommissioned in 1961. The owner, Hamburg Water Works (HWW), used the tower until 1970 for its archives and as a maintenance shop, even as the building slowly decayed from inattention. Its annual maintenance costs were about DM 30,000 (US$8,235). The waterworks considered a series of proposals for adaptive use: among them a mausoleum for 30,000 cremation urns, a multilevel car-park structure, and an archives building for the University of Hamburg. HWW concluded that the only way to justify its continued ownership of the tower would be to turn the building into its administrative center. But the tower could not be retrofitted with enough space for HWW's 500 employees, necessitating a 4,000-square-meter (43,056-sf) addition. This proposal unleashed an uproar led by the activist Green Party, and HWW eventually withdrew its proposal.

In 1989, HWW put the water tower up for sale for private development with the following conditions: redevelopment must not require public subsidy; only noncommercial uses were permitted; cost-free public use of the completed development must be permitted at least half the time; and the property and development rights could not be resold for the first five years. HWW received 15 offers, the most convincing one from Munich investor Ernst Joachim Storr, who paid DM 39,200 (US$22,937) for the development rights in 1990. The water tower stood undeveloped for a five-year period, after which Storr renegotiated the development terms, for a DM 2 million (US$1.4 million) payment, rescinding the original restrictions.

The renegotiation allowed use to shift to a hotel, at which point Patrizia Immobilien AG's development arm became interested. Patrizia took some years to find a partner hotel as operator. In 2003, Patrizia formed a joint venture with Ernst Joachim Storr and contracted a leasehold agreement with the Mövenpick Hotel & Resorts chain.

The water tower is on the edge of Sternschanzen Park, a park built in 1863 on the grounds of a star-shaped fortress (hence the park's name) outside the old city walls of Hamburg. The immediate neighborhood, also called the Schanzen district, now is a hip community of mixed residential and retail uses. Three subway and surface rail lines serve the neighborhood; across the street is the Hamburg Trade Fair grounds (40 exhibitions and 1 million visitors per year); 450 meters (1,476 ft) farther to the east—on the opposite side of the Planten un Blomen park—is the Hamburg Congress Centre (200 conventions and 200,000 attendees per year); in the midst of the Trade Fair grounds stands the Heinrich Hertz communications tower at a height of 280 meters (918 ft).

The project took four years to complete. The damaged octagonal roof had been removed already. The interior was entirely gutted, with demolished materials lifted out, piecemeal, by crane. The exterior shell was reinforced from the inside, and a concrete shell was poured within the outer brick walls, which thicken to 1.5 meters (five ft) at the original foundation. Fourteen above-grade and two below-grade levels were inserted within the tower itself. Finally came a new octagonal cone roof, identical in profile to the old one, but now with dormer-style and observatory windows for the four new levels under the conical roof.

Two additions to the original tower completed the project. A 222 square-meter (2,390-sf) glazed addition adds meeting rooms and two levels of underground parking (44 spaces). And a grand entrance at the street, 25 meters (82 ft) away, permits guests to enter the hotel and take a subterranean escalator to the center of the lobby area at the tower's base. This underground tube satisfies the development requirement that no part of the project cut off any part of the park from free public access. The only expansion of the tower's footprint in the park is the meeting room addition and 40 surface parking spaces at the base of the tower, all within the 0.57-hectare (1.4-ac) parcel.

PROJECT DATA

Website
www.wasserturm-schanzenpark.de

Site Area
0.57 ha (1.4 ac)

Facilities
1,681 m² (18,094 sf) commercial and
    restaurant space
226 hotel rooms
84 parking spaces

Land Uses
hotel, restaurant, parking

Start/Completion Dates
December 2004–June 2007

PHOTOGRAPHS BY PATRIZIA IMMOBILIEN AG

Pall Italia Building

BUCCINASCO, ITALY

The Pall Italia Building is located in an industrial area of Buccinasco, Italy, a municipality seven kilometers (4.3 mi) southwest of Milan. The new Italian headquarters of the Pall Corporation, a U.S.-based global company specializing in the filtration, separation, and purification of fluids for the medical and industrial fields, consists of 3,463 square meters (37,275 sf) of office space and 3,513 square meters (37,814 sf) of research laboratories on an 8.8-hectare (21.8-ac) site. One of Italy's first green buildings, the Pall Italia Building uses a range of sustainable technologies—thermal-resistant façades, innovative daylighting techniques, and renewable energy—to achieve zero on-site carbon emissions.

Designed by the Milan-based Progetto CMR–Massimo Roj Architects, Italy's largest architecture firm, the new Pall Italia headquarters is divided into three buildings roughly paralleling each other—two are newly constructed; the third is a refurbished two-level structure—each with a distinct function: Building A consists of the corporate offices, Building B is home to the life sciences laboratories,

DEVELOPMENT TEAM

Owner/Developer
Pall Italia Srl.
Buccinasco, Italy
www.pall.com

Design Architect
Progetto CMR–Massimo Roj
  Architects
Milan, Italy
www.progettocmr.com

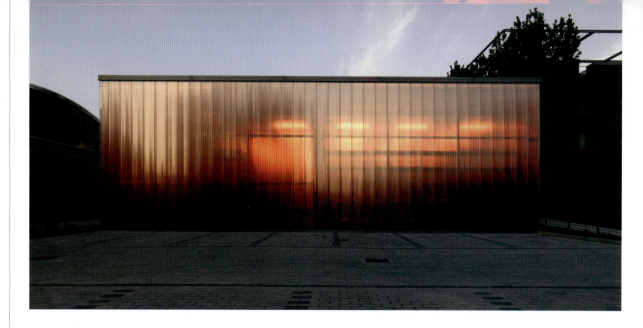

Website
www.pall.com

Site Area
8.8 ha (21.8 ac)

Facilities
3,463 m² (37,275 sf) office
3,513 m² (37,814 sf) industrial
81 surface parking space

Land Uses
office, industrial/warehouse, parking

Start/Completion Dates
2004–September 2007

and Building C hosts the industrial research space. The three structures are connected by an elevated, two-level glass walkway.

The three-story Building A, which fronts Via Emilia, the main road, contains offices for the corporate headquarters. The structure features slender metal framing and a glass curtain wall, with ventilated cement-fiber cladding on the east and west ends of the building. The long, south-facing street façade integrates a "light shelf" system: light-gray metal slats block the direct sunrays while reflecting natural light deep into the building. The continuous glazed curtain wall reduces solar heat gain and is equipped on each floor with external maintenance walkways. The roof at Pall Italia's corporate headquarters is crowned with a lightweight, gridded steel structure capable of supporting photovoltaic panels.

The flexible design of the interior space permits an extension of the building's life cycle beyond its current use. With a partition wall system, the office layout can be reconfigured quickly and easily. The modern interior is open and uncluttered, allowing the ample natural light to penetrate.

Building B consists of two above-ground floors containing laboratories with a warehouse at ground level. It is separated from Building A by a shallow pool, 8.5 meters (28 ft) wide by 55 meters (180 ft) long, that runs the length of the office building. The translucent building envelope features alveolar polycarbonate panels, providing elevated thermal resistance while maximizing the interior natural light. The end bay of this building houses the technical and mechanical equipment for the entire complex. The renovated Building C is used for storage on the ground floor and has research space for the industrial sector in the upper floors.

At the Pall Italia Building, Progetto CMR applied a number of green building techniques: the complex is oriented toward the south, maximizing exposure to the sun's path; the use of a reversible hydrothermal heat pump for heating and cooling reduces energy usage by 50 percent; and photovoltaic panels provide electric cogeneration.

Well-suited for its high-tech occupant, the Pall Italia Building is functional, flexible, and efficient. Completed in September 2007, the high-performance project boasts zero on-site carbon emissions because of its reliance on solar and geothermal/hydrothermal energy, and the extensive daylighting and efficient heating and cooling systems allow the Pall Italia Building to consume significantly less energy than a comparable structure.

PHOTOGRAPHS BY PROGETTO CMR–
MASSIMO ROJ ARCHITECTS

59

Złote Tarasy

WARSAW, POLAND

The landmark destination in Warsaw's newest high-rise district, Złote Tarasy is a state-of-the-art, 225,000-square-meter (2.4 million-sf) commercial complex on a 3.2-hectare (7.9-ac) infill site. Złote Tarasy's trademark element is its one-hectare (2.5-ac) undulating glass roof—inspired by the tree canopies that shade Warsaw's historic parks—that encloses its lively retail and entertainment plaza. Visited by more than 1.3 million people a month, the center consists of 45,000 square meters (484,376 sf) of office space, more than 200 shops, 30 restaurants, and an eight-screen cinema.

Złote Tarasy is designed to reconnect the project area—formerly a massive surface parking lot—to the city and to realize the site's potential as the center of a large urban system. Since the end of World War II, the underused parcel has served as a parking lot and bus platform for the adjacent Central Railway Station. As a result, the main transportation hub of Warsaw remained detached from the expanding central business district, severing two integral parts of the urban core.

DEVELOPMENT TEAM

Owners/Developers
ING Real Estate Development
Warsaw, Poland
www.ingrealestate.com

Złote Tarasy Sp. z o.o.
Warsaw, Poland
www.zlotetarasy.pl

Design Architect
The Jerde Partnership
Venice, California
www.jerde.com

Associate Architect
Epstein Sp. z o.o.
Warsaw, Poland
www.epstein-isi.com

PROJECT DATA

Website
www.zlotetarasy.pl

Site Area
3.2 ha (7.9 ac)

Facilities
63,500 m² (683,508 sf) retail
45,000 m² (484,376 sf) office

Land Uses
retail, restaurants, entertainment,
office, parks/open space,
structured parking

Start/Completion Dates
November 2002–August 2007

In 1998, ING Real Estate Development, the developer of Złote Tarasy, and the city of Warsaw began a joint venture to revitalize the project area and return coherence to the city center. The public partner made the land contribution in the form of the vacant parking area, and ING Real Estate Development financed the investment, developed and constructed the project, and now manages the entire complex. The Jerde Partnership—known for its hyperanimated shopping centers—led the design team.

Złote Tarasy was designed to acknowledge the city's rich cultural history while also projecting a distinct architectural vernacular for the future. Inspired by the city's historic park system, which forms a centuries-old ribbon of green space through downtown, the project establishes 6,000 square meters (64,583 sf) of urban park space, including an 80-year-old red oak, greenery on the internal and external terraces and roofs, and water features.

The enclosed retail plaza—comprising 63,500 square meters (683,508 sf) of shops, restaurants, and entertainment venues—is organized into terraces, which allow visitors to overlook the activities in the interior courtyard and outdoor piazza. The open-air public square, situated in front of the retail complex, provides sidewalk seating for the center's many restaurants and space for concerts, shows, and exhibitions.

Złote Tarasy is framed by the Class A mid- and high-rise office towers that surround the shopping area to the north and east. The orientation of the buildings takes advantage of the natural solar path, permitting sunlight to reach the interiors of the work space, and mechanized louvers respond to the position of the sun to regulate temperature. The curvilinear office buildings encircle the covered plaza, responding with a shape and concept that reflect the circular green boulevard originally planned in the central part of the city.

The greatest architectural and engineering task was the design and construction of the undulating glass roof. The project's signature feature spans a full hectare (2.5 ac) over the expansive retail plaza, infusing the interior with natural light and protecting visitors from Warsaw's harsh winters. The impressive structure is composed of nearly 5,000 custom-shaped triangular panes of glass that fit into a self-supporting steel geodesic structure.

The project had to overcome a number of administrative challenges on its path to completion, including lengthy regulatory procedures, construction delays, and protests from one environmental association. Ultimately, the environmental claim was dismissed by Polish courts as unfounded; however, the accumulated issues conspired to delay the project. Even so, it eventually opened to great fanfare in July 2007.

One of the first developers in Poland after the country achieved independence in 1989, ING Real Estate Development—through Złote Tarasy—helped found the model for public/private development cooperation in Warsaw. In fact, no legislation covered the complex character of the public/private partnership at the time. Only in 2005, in the middle of Złote Tarasy's construction, was the necessary legal framework established to govern the process. The pioneering project has also been a financial success: it was 100 percent leased upon completion.

MIXED USE

Atelier|505

BOSTON, MASSACHUSETTS

The product of a ground-breaking public/private partnership, Atelier|505 is a mixed-use development in Boston's South End that includes 103 luxury condominiums, 20,776 square feet (1,930 m²) of ground-floor retail, and a performing arts facility. The 300,118-square-foot (27,882-m²) project complements the adjacent Cyclorama theater, forming a truly integrated "arts block" for the city of Boston. Using a financial model that has been studied by developers, urban planners, and city officials, the Druker Company partnered with the city of Boston, the Boston Center for the Arts (BCA), and the Huntington Theatre Company to create a vibrant hub of activity in a rising neighborhood.

JURY STATEMENT

A partnership among a developer, the city, and two arts institutions has transformed a contaminated, irregular lot in an underinvested area of Boston's South End into a mixed-use block that is returning life to surrounding streets. The creative financing arrangement allowed the for-profit, 103-unit condominium and street-level retail core to pay for the shell construction of a 550-seat theater complex, providing the city with its first new performing arts venue in over 70 years.

DEVELOPMENT TEAM

Owner/Developer
The Druker Company, Ltd.
Boston, Massachusetts

Design Architect
Machado and Silvetti Associates, Inc.
Boston, Massachusetts
www.machado-silvetti.com

Managing Architect
ADD, Inc.
Cambridge, Massachusetts
www.addinc.com

In the 1960s, the city of Boston ground-leased a large parcel in Boston's South End to the BCA. The organization was able to operate several of the buildings on the property, including a small theater, with moderate success, but the small nonprofit lacked the budgetary capacity to take full advantage of the land. As the underused parcel lay dormant for decades, the need for a modern, medium-sized performing arts facility in Boston intensified. In 1997, the city recommended a novel solution: a design competition in which participating developers would propose a use for the property that would be profitable enough to support the construction of a performing arts complex at no cost to the BCA.

To make the funding of the arts center viable, the developer understood that condominium sale prices would need to exceed even those in the priciest Boston markets—a risky proposition in the emerging South End neighborhood. However, planning luxury, high-end condominiums allowed the developer to offer the city a more generous financial package than its competitors: in addition to building the core and shell of the performing arts center, the Druker Company was able to provide a $2 million endowment to the BCA.

In early 1998, the Druker Company was selected to develop the site, based on the design concept of architects Machado and Silvetti Associates, and in association with the managing architect, ADD,

Inc. To reach the profit threshold required to subsidize the performing arts facility, Atelier|505 needed to be developed on a large scale. However, the 1.2-acre (0.5-ha) site is situated in a smaller-scale neighborhood—the nation's largest historic Victorian rowhouse district, consisting mainly of two- or three-story townhouses. Reconciling this contrast in scale became one of the design team's chief challenges.

To avoid overwhelming the neighborhood, the architects designed a building that appears as four distinct elements, each relating to its environment. For instance, where the building faces a quiet residential street, it steps down to four stories, mimicking the massing and style of the adjacent townhouses. In turn, the most imposing façade stands at the busy corner of the broad Tremont and Berkeley streets, establishing a commanding yet appropriate presence in the low-rise neighborhood.

Although a contemporary structure, Atelier|505 was designed within the architectural context of the surrounding neighborhood in regard to form, material, and fenestration. The use of mansard roofs, red-brick construction, and masonry openings pays homage to the Victorian architecture of the South End Landmark District without resorting to faux-historic construction. The result is a decidedly modern building that still manages to integrate seamlessly into the historic community.

PHOTOGRAPHS BY ANTON GRASSL (66, 67, 68L, 71L); ROBERT BENSON (68R, 69); THE DRUKER COMPANY, LTD. (70); LUCY CHEN (71R)

SITE PLAN

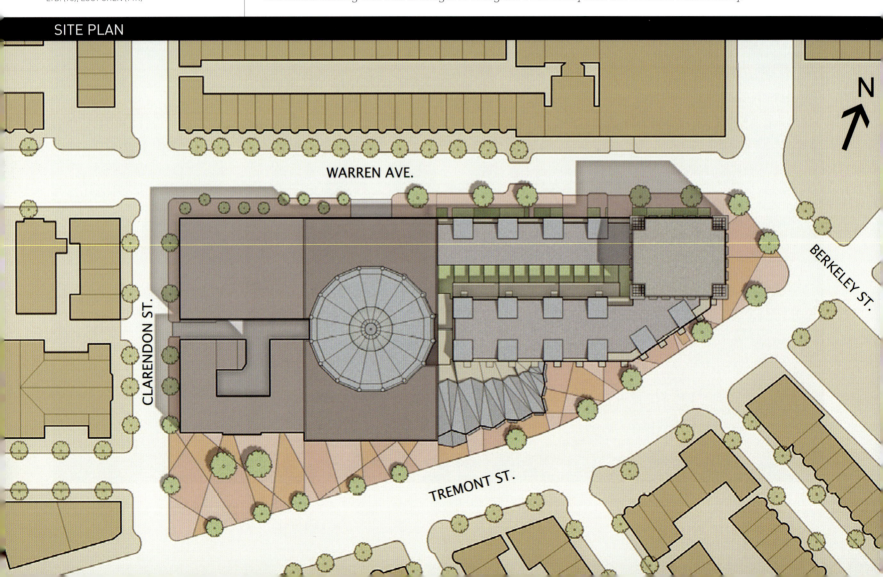

Providing the city of Boston with its first new performing arts theaters in more than 70 years, the 51,019-square-foot (4,740-m²) Calderwood Pavilion is composed of two separate, state-of-the-art facilities—a formal 350-seat proscenium theater and a flexible 200-seat "black box" theater. The complex also includes rehearsal rooms, classrooms, offices, and other support spaces and shares service and public areas with the Victorian-age Cyclorama next door.

In addition to the risk associated with selling luxury condominiums in an unproven market, Atelier|505 faced environmental and community challenges. The project team encountered larger-than-expected contamination issues: the presence of volatile organic compounds, mercury, and lead were all discovered at elevated levels. Working with the Boston Redevelopment Authority on the remediation effort, the Druker Company contributed approximately $2 million toward the cleanup.

An active and vocal community association initially opposed the development, concerned that the size and activity of the mixed-use complex would degrade the character of the neighborhood. Although more than two years were necessary to resolve the parking, traffic, and access issues with the city of Boston, the project ultimately solved many of the problems it was presumed to exacerbate—for example, the district's chronic parking shortage has been eased by the 350-space parking garage.

From an economic standpoint, every component of Atelier|505 has been a success. The 103 luxury condominiums sold out prior to construction at record prices for the South End, resulting in a residential return on total cost of approximately 35 percent. The ground-floor retail and restaurants are fully leased above pro forma rents, with a lively mix of local, national, and international tenants. The exceptional returns on the for-profit components provided the necessary funds for the 550-seat theater complex, which opened in October 2004 to critical and public acclaim.

PROJECT DATA

Site Area
1.2 ac (0.5 ha)

Facilities
20,776 sf (1,930 m²) retail
51,019 sf (4,740 m²) performing
  arts space
103 multifamily units
350 structured parking spaces

Land Uses
residential, retail, restaurant,
  entertainment, educational,
  structured parking

Start/Completion Dates
June 2002–August 2004

Beijing Finance Street

BEIJING, CHINA

Since Beijing was awarded the 2008 Summer Olympics three years ago, the capital city has undergone a physical transformation on a massive scale. At the center of the enormous, citywide development effort lies Beijing Finance Street—a 3.36 million-square-meter (36.2 million-sf) mixed-use development that features offices, luxury hotels, retail space, and apartments arranged around a meandering central park. The CNY31.6 billion (US$4.6 billion) project is situated on the former site of a dilapidated *hutong* neighborhood—a cluster of narrow alleys lined by traditional courtyard residences—five blocks west of the Forbidden City, Beijing's historic center.

DEVELOPMENT TEAM

Owner/Developer
Beijing Financial Street
  Holding Co., Ltd.
Beijing, China
www.jrjkg.com.cn

Design Architect/Master Planner
Skidmore, Owings & Merrill, LLP
San Francisco, California
www.som.com

Landscape Architect
SWA Group
San Francisco, California
www.swagroup.com

JURY STATEMENT

Just blocks from the Forbidden City, Beijing Finance Street establishes a new nerve center for China's booming economy. This city within a city—35 city blocks organized along a central, meandering green space—creates a new, influential model for the country with a sustainable and transit-oriented mixed-use district for the financial leadership of China.

As Beijing has boomed, little has been done to preserve public space and landscaped areas for its ever-increasing population. Urban life in China has traditionally taken place in open, communal spaces; however, government-sponsored planning efforts have interrupted the urban fabric, creating megablocks and stratifying uses across the capital city. Much of the new development has been constructed within this framework, resulting in uninspired, hulking buildings drawn back and isolated from the street.

The architecture firm of Skidmore, Owings & Merrill (SOM)—awarded the project after winning an international design competition hosted by the developer, Financial Street Holding Co.—sought to reverse this trend. SOM's master plan draws on tradition, where outdoor areas are extensions of the indoor realm: for instance, building façades are punctuated with openings to interior courtyards, a concept reminiscent of the ancient *hutong* community that once settled here. The project's boundary is porous and intersected by many paths and connections, which attracts visitors to the district and encourages interchange between the development and the surrounding neighborhoods.

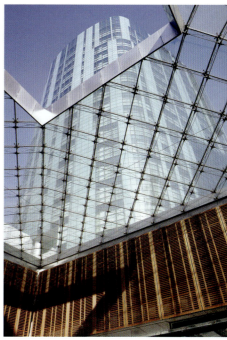

At Beijing Finance Street, sleek, modern buildings toe the sidewalk, introducing a vibrant street wall that encourages pedestrian activity. Working with the landscape architecture firm of SWA Group, the team designed a curving, narrow park at the core of the project, with a network of small gardens and courtyards interwoven throughout the buildings. All the structures are connected by an underground roadway, where cars and trucks travel out of the way of pedestrians. The offices are clustered along the noisy periphery of the project site, whereas the condominiums and shops face the peaceful, landscaped interior.

The majority of the project's 18 buildings house 751,000 square meters (8.1 million sf) of office space, principally devoted to the finance and banking sector. Almost all important decisions about Chinese finance are incubated and executed in this 35-block district, where the country's highest financial strategy and regulatory offices are located, including the People's Bank of China, China's Banking Regulatory Commission, and China's Securities Regulatory Commission. Beijing Finance Street also reflects China's turn toward a market economy—earning it the moniker the "Wall Street

of the East"—because it is home to more than a thousand private financial institutions, such as UBS, Goldman Sachs, JP Morgan, and Bank of America.

The heart of the project is formed by the 63,500-square-meter (683,508-sf) retail building and central park. A glass roof 259 meters (850 ft) long covers the crescent-shaped shopping center. Four terraces of shops and restaurants encircle the interior, and ground-floor cafés and shops wrap the building exterior, spilling out into the green space and plazas.

The mixed-use development also incorporates principles of sustainability: the site is oriented to optimize daylighting and natural ventilation advantages; the below-grade travelways reduce traffic congestion; building façades integrate high-performance strategies; and all residential units are heated by geothermal systems.

Beijing Finance Street—a model of sustainable design and mixed-use development in China—has created a memorable urban district firmly rooted in Beijing's long history while becoming a world-renowned financial center. The project has buoyed real estate values in the surrounding area, and financial institutions have flocked to the business district from around the world.

PROJECT DATA

Website
www.jrjkg.com.cn

Site Area
31 ha (77 ac)

Facilities
751,000 m² (8.1 million sf) office
63,500 m² (683,508 sf) retail
300 single-family units (approximate)
600 hotel rooms (approximate)
8,620 parking spaces

Land Uses
office, retail, residential, restaurant, hotel, civic, parks/open space

Start/Completion Dates
January 2002–September 2007

SITE PLAN

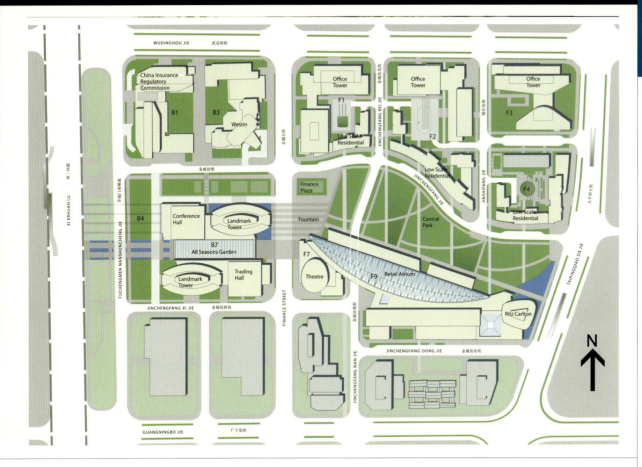

PHOTOGRAPHS BY TIM GRIFFITH (72, 73, 74L, 74-75C, 75R, 76TL, 76BL, 76R); GERALD RATTO (77)

Clipper Mill

BALTIMORE, MARYLAND

Clipper Mill converts a long underused 17.5-acre (7.1-ha) site that once housed Maryland's largest and most productive machine manufacturing complex into a vibrant, mixed-use community. The development team reused the 1853 historic site and its five deteriorating buildings to create 61,500 square feet (5,714 m²) of office space, 47,500 square feet (4,413 m²) of studio space for artists and craftspeople, and a wide range of housing, including 34 townhouses, 38 semidetached houses, and 62 condominium and 36 rental apartments. Completed in September 2006, Clipper Mill

DEVELOPMENT TEAM

Owners/Developers
Struever Bros. Eccles & Rouse
Baltimore, Maryland
www.sber.com

Clipper Redevelopment
 Company, LLC
Baltimore, Maryland

Millrace Building LLC
Baltimore, Maryland

Clipper for Sale LLC
Baltimore, Maryland

Architect
Cho Benn Holback + Associates, Inc.
Baltimore, Maryland
www.cbhassociates.com

Landscape Architect
Mahan Rykiel Associates, Inc.
Baltimore, Maryland
www.mahanrykiel.com

JURY STATEMENT

A midtown site that once housed a major contributor to Baltimore's industrial economy has been transformed into a mixed-use complex of artisan space, offices, and residences. Taking advantage of the property's location next to a light-rail transit stop and adjacent to an extensive hiking trail network that the developer enhanced along its adjoining portions, Clipper Mill restored the historical characteristics of the property while introducing progressive sustainability features.

is a transit-oriented community that integrates many elements of sustainable development. It offers a unique sense of place that is created in part by the preservation of the site's history and the incorporation of the work of resident craftspeople into the project's design.

When developer Struever Bros. Eccles & Rouse (SBER) took on the $88 million, three-phase project, a number of artists and craftspeople lived and worked on site. SBER wanted to provide safe, code-compliant, and affordable studio space for resident artists; preserve the charm of the historically significant site, which contained five buildings in varying states of disrepair; and convert the complex into a viable mixed-use community that would attract families from outside the city of Baltimore. Its goal was not just to rehabilitate the property but also to inspire the neighborhood.

The project faced numerous challenges. A number of underground obstructions—both natural and constructed—were uncovered. Unforeseen structural problems in several buildings resulted in budget overruns. A neighbor and a tenant launched a project-delaying lawsuit using false deeds to claim ownership of the land. Moreover, market conditions forced one building to be changed from 83 rental apartments to 62 condominiums after the foundation and first-floor concrete decking had been poured.

The financing package was complex and multilayered, involving tax increment financing, federal and state historic-preservation tax credits enhanced by new market tax credits, developer and joint

SITE PLAN

venture partner equity, and grant funds from the Maryland Department of the Environment's brown-field incentive program. The site required approximately $1.2 million in environmental remediation to remove contaminated soils, asbestos insulation, lead paint, and underground oil storage tanks. The project's on-site utility infrastructure was developed in partnership with the city of Baltimore, whose public works department provided specifications and design guidance.

The integration of sustainable features was an important goal. Antique steel beams, stones, and sprocket wheels from the original machine shop were recycled as parts of the building structure, landscaping features, and architectural centerpieces. A 1,600-square-foot (149-m²) green roof forms the floor of the open-air atrium of one of the residential structures, lowering temperatures in the building and reducing and purifying stormwater runoff. A porous paving system was used for an office parking lot, which filters stormwater and allows it to infiltrate the groundwater system rather than discharging directly into a nearby river. Clipper Mill's most innovative green feature is a living wall—the first in the United States—that filters air through plants before returning it to the heating, ventilating, and air-conditioning system. The wall is in a structure that once served as stables and that is now used as a design studio by Biohabitats, an environmental consultant.

Finally, with a light-rail stop at the entrance and shuttle service to other modes of public transit, Clipper Mill offers residents, commercial tenants, and visitors a range of transportation options, thus reducing their reliance on automobiles.

PROJECT DATA

Website
www.clippermill.net

Site Area
17.5 ac (7.1 ha)

Facilities
61,500 sf (5,714 m²) office
3,500 sf (325 m²) retail
72 single-family units
98 multifamily units
375 surface parking spaces

Land Uses
office, residential, retail, restaurant,
   recreation, parking, open space

Start/Completion Dates
June 2004–September 2006

General Motors Renaissance Center

DETROIT, MICHIGAN

In the mid-1990s, General Motors (GM) began scouting locations for a new global headquarters. The automaking giant initially considered a suburban location, following the trend set by many Detroit-based companies, or retrofitting its existing New Center facilities, located five miles (8.05 km) north of downtown.

But in 1996, GM opted to undertake the bold and symbolic step of returning to downtown, initiating a radical makeover of the 5.5 million-square-foot (510,967-m²) GM Renaissance Center, representing one of North America's most extensive and massive renovations ever completed. The new GM Renaissance Center—a complex of seven interconnected skyscrapers—has reintroduced the notoriously isolated megastructure to downtown Detroit, providing a connection to the central city and the revitalized waterfront.

Originally completed in 1977 by the Ford Company, the $337 million complex once stood as the largest private development in the world. Four 39-story towers ring the 74-floor central skyscraper, which remains the tallest hotel in the Western hemisphere, with two additional high-rise buildings to the east. The original Renaissance Center was intended to help revitalize the flagging Detroit economy; however, the complex by itself was unable to stem the exodus of people and businesses to the suburbs. As offices, stores, and restaurants shuttered their doors in downtown, the Renaissance Center became marooned along the waterfront.

The architectural and urban design flaws of the original Renaissance Center also contributed to the project's inability to reverse disinvestment in downtown Detroit. Critics accused the megastructure of being "a city within a city," bunkered by 35-foot (10.67-m) berms and encircled by elevated highways. Internally, a repetitive circular geometry proved disorienting for visitors and employees, and the complex lacked any connection to the adjacent Detroit River. By 1983, the project had defaulted on its mortgage twice and had become the icon for the urban decline of the once great city.

DEVELOPMENT TEAM

Owner
General Motors Corporation
Detroit, Michigan
www.gm.com

Developer of Redevelopment
Hines
Houston, Texas
www.hines.com

Architect of Redevelopment
Skidmore, Owings & Merrill LLP
Chicago, Illinois
www.som.com

JURY STATEMENT

Automaker General Motors consolidated its seven suburban office locations—signaling the corporation's commitment to downtown Detroit—by repurposing the 1970s-era multistory Renaissance Center into its world headquarters. By turning around a reminder of Detroit's decline and returning 10,000 employees to downtown, GM has reintegrated the complex into the city fabric and invited the public to the riverfront with its green spaces and promenades.

When GM purchased the Renaissance Center in 1996 for $75 million, one-third of the complex was vacant. Through a request for proposals process, the automaking giant selected Skidmore, Owings & Merrill (SOM) to renovate the aging towers and dated, disconnected interior space. The rehabilitation of the Renaissance Center focused on reacquainting the complex with the urban environment and a long-ignored amenity: the Detroit River. To accomplish the former, the design team began by demolishing the three-story berms—the symbol of the Renaissance Center's former life as a corporate compound—that housed the heating, ventilating, and air-conditioning and generator systems. The elevated vehicular driveway was removed and a pavilion 30 feet (9.1 m) high and 30 feet (9.1 m) wide with glass curtain walls was constructed in its place, bringing the entrance to street level. The glass and cable structure reflects GM's industrial past and establishes a distinct "front door"—a feature the labyrinthine fortress previously lacked.

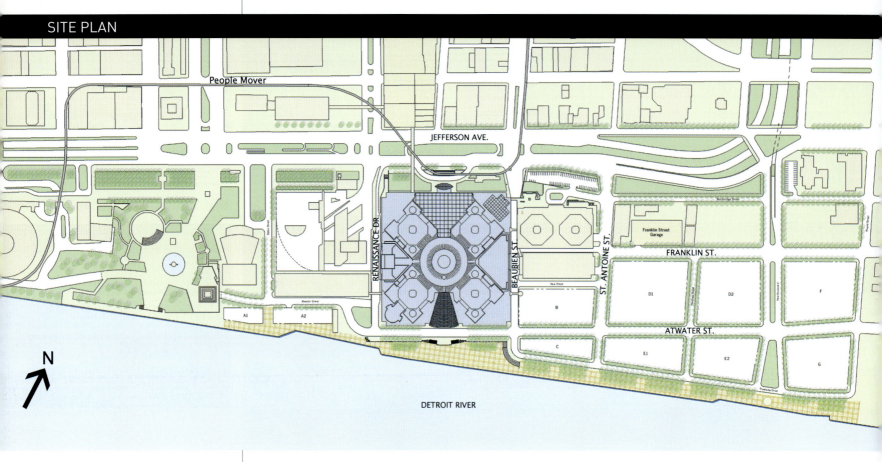

N

PHOTOGRAPHS BY SKIDMORE, OWINGS, & MERRILL
LLP & JUSTIN MACONOCHIE, HEDRICH BLESSING
(84, 86, 87L, 87TR, 87BR, 89L); SKIDMORE, OWINGS, &
MERRILL LLP (88); HINES (89R)

The newly constructed Wintergarden, a five-story atrium cut into the original podium, connects the Renaissance Center with the riverfront. The fan-shaped space brings the south side of the site to grade with the river, and its glass face allows natural light to penetrate the atrium and lobby. With its glass skylights and expansive vertical space, the Wintergarden houses multiple shops and cafés and provides both visual and physical connection with the Detroit River. Additionally, the space has held more than 200 social events every year, ranging from hosting charity functions to acting as the media headquarters for Super Bowl XL.

Encouraged by the city's renewed interest in the riverfront, in 2004, GM completed its section of the Detroit River Walk, a 5.5-mile (8.9-km) lineal park along the river. The promenade stretches from the Ambassador Bridge to Bell Island, connecting the riverfront section of downtown and complementing areas designated for urban redevelopment. Previously surface parking, the south-facing section of the Renaissance Center now opens onto a vibrant plaza, linking the project with the rest of the waterfront development along downtown.

The drab interior space of the Renaissance Center had long been maligned as confusing and disorienting; for example, the four office towers GM planned to occupy were not directly connected to each other. To rectify these design flaws, SOM, the lead architect and master planner for the project,

introduced a modern, glass circulation ring within the central atrium. Bridges branch off the suspended walkway, connecting visitors and employees to the four office towers, the Wintergarden, GM University, and the main lobby. Twelve feet (3.7 m) wide, the illuminated circulation ring contrasts favorably with the concrete interior.

In addition to the Renaissance Center renovations, SOM drew up the River East Master Plan that addresses GM's surplus property: 140 acres (56.7 ha) of riverfront land directly adjacent to its global headquarters. The plan calls for a primarily residential, mixed-use neighborhood to link the Renaissance Center with the burgeoning development downtown. In 2007, Hines partnered with GM to develop the first six acres (2.4 ha) of the tract, which fronts the Detroit River directly east of GM's new global headquarters. The Houston-based developer's initial plans call for two luxury condominium towers and a townhouse project, each designed to take advantage of the premier waterfront location and the amenities offered at the GM Renaissance Center.

PROJECT DATA

Website
www.gmrencen.com

Site Area
152 ac (62 ha)

Facilities
2.3 million sf (213,677 m²) office
230,000 sf (21,368 m²) retail
1,300 single-family units (proposed)
1,298 hotel rooms
2,385 surface parking spaces

Land Uses
office, retail, hotel, residential, civic,
 restaurant, recreation, education,
 parking, open space

Start/Completion Dates
1996–2007

National Ballet School of Canada/Radio City

TORONTO, CANADA

After the Canadian Broadcast Corporation relocated its English-language broadcasting headquarters from this historic Toronto neighborhood in 1997, the land and buildings sat vacant for several years. Formerly home to a 152-meter (499-ft) radio tower, offices, and performance space, the one-hectare (2.4-ac) site—located in the dense rental market of Church/

JURY STATEMENT

In a creative partnership—the National Ballet School of Canada, the Canadian Broadcasting Corporation, the city, and a local developer—multiple easements, transfers of development rights, and complex ownership structures have allowed the rehabilitation and reuse of heritage buildings; construction of new residential, academic, and performance facilities for one of the premier ballet schools in the world; public urban spaces; and 414 residential units in 18 townhouses and two residential towers.

DEVELOPMENT TEAM

Owners/Developers
National Ballet School of Canada
Toronto, Canada
www.nationalballetschool.org

Context Development, Inc.
Toronto, Canada
www.context.ca

Design Architects
Kuwabara Payne McKenna Blumberg
   Architects
Toronto, Canada
www.kpmb.com

architectsAlliance
Toronto, Canada
www.architectsalliance.com

Master Planner
Goldsmith Borgal & Company
   Limited Architects
Toronto, Canada
www.gbca.ca

Urban Planner
Urban Strategies, Inc.
Toronto, Canada
www.urbanstrategies.com

Wellesley Village—now consists of 32,516 square meters (350,000 sf) of condominium space, 18 townhouses, and a 16,723-square-meter (180,000-sf) arts training institute.

Context Development, Inc., purchased the site in 2000 and, in conjunction with the National Ballet School of Canada (NBS), structured a deal that allowed the NBS to purchase roughly half the land—on which it would restore two historic buildings and construct a new school—for the nominal fee of CAN$1. The city then granted Context the density transfers it needed for the financially feasible development of 18 townhouses and two high-rise condominium towers, with underground garages on

the remainder of the site. The result is an innovative, high-density, urban infill residential project connected to a new, state-of-the-art NBS complex via two landscaped courtyards.

Context's master plan established an irregular property line that split the site in two, with the ballet school sited on the Jarvis Street side of the property and the residential component occupying the Mutual Street side. The rezoning and planning approval were filed in a single application, yielding a number of design synergies, such as shared easements for the public lane and single-ramp access to the underground parking. The NBS campus consists of a modern, three-story training center threaded between two heritage buildings—an 1856 late-Georgian residence and an 1898/1901 academic building. The transparency of the vertical campus reduces the perceived density of the structure and animates the street wall by showcasing the activities of the students.

Most of Radio City's 414 residential units are located in two slender high-rise towers—the 25-story North Tower and the 30-story South Tower. The structures' unusually small floor plates—650 square meters (6,997 sf)—and their placement, situated deep within the site, minimize their apparent bulk and do not disturb the residential scale of surrounding side streets. Positioning the towers diagonally to each other and installing floor-to-ceiling windows in every unit maximize views and increase the marketability for the condominium project. Sharing a contractor facilitated communication, created economies of scale, and allowed the use of common construction materials; the use of identical steel,

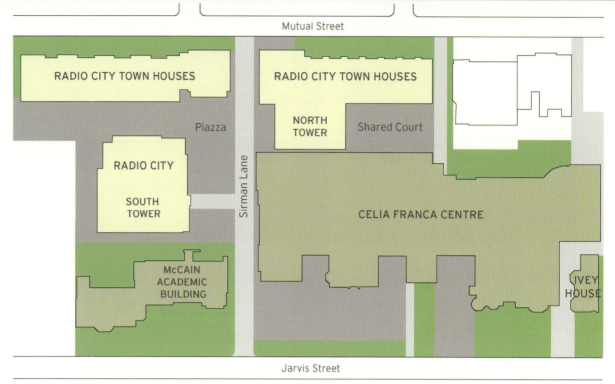

Mutual Street

RADIO CITY TOWN HOUSES

RADIO CITY TOWN HOUSES

Piazza

NORTH TOWER

Shared Court

Sirman Lane

RADIO CITY

SOUTH TOWER

CELIA FRANCA CENTRE

McCAIN ACADEMIC BUILDING

IVEY HOUSE

Jarvis Street

Entrance Lanes, Walkways
Courtyards, Forecourts
Green Space, Landscape
Radio City
National Ballet School

 N

PROJECT DATA

Website
http://www.radiocitycondo.com

Site Area
1.0 ha (2.4 ac)

Facilities
16,723 m² (180,000 sf) arts training
  facility
372 m² (4,000 sf) retail/
  entertainment space
414 multifamily units
18 single-family units

Land Uses
residential, retail, entertainment,
  education, parks/open space

Start/Completion Dates
June 2003–June 2007

glass, and concrete in both the Radio City towers and NBS campus presents a unifying aesthetic for the entire project.

Fronting Mutual Street, the three-story townhouses echo the rooflines and form of the adjacent Victorian rowhouses. The façade of the townhomes is covered in light-yellow brick—a common building material in the city—and each unit includes a single-car garage. The arrangement of the buildings creates an interior piazza enlivened with public art, while a shared courtyard connects the townhouse component to the NBS complex.

Like many urban infill developments, the project ran into a major roadblock along the way to completion. During the excavation process, an underground stream was discovered directly below the site of the North Tower. Dewatering took six months, and a portion of the underground parking garage was eliminated from the plans to avoid any environmental impact on the river system.

The project responds to pent-up demand for for-sale housing from the area's hip, upwardly mobile residents. Because the village also is the heart of Toronto's gay community, Context geared its marketing efforts almost exclusively to these prospective homebuyers, and more than 90 percent of Radio City purchasers ultimately came from this demographic group.

Launched in May 2001 and substantially completed in June 2007, the CAN$85 million (US$84 million) project is a clear financial success. Both towers sold out quickly, and resale values continue to climb, outperforming most of the surrounding market. Overall, Radio City has benefited the community greatly, both by introducing new housing that replaced vacant land and empty buildings and by enabling the NBS to construct a new school in conjunction with the restoration of historic structures.

According to Howard Cohen, president of Context Development, "Radio City was an exciting opportunity to help transform a decrepit piece of land in Toronto's downtown core into a vibrant, mixed-use project. The success of Radio City lies in that it has provided much-needed residential density alongside a new home for the National Ballet School of Canada."

PHOTOGRAPHS BY CONTEXT DEVELOPMENT, INC.
(90, 94); TOM ARBAN (91, 93L, 93R); EDUARD HUEBER
(92, 95)

Tokyo Midtown

TOKYO, JAPAN

Tokyo Midtown is an urban infill project on the 6.9-hectare (17-ac) former headquarters site of the Defense Agency, a cabinet-level ministry of the Japanese government, in the Roppongi district of the capital city. The project includes a 248-meter (814-ft) skyscraper surrounded by five buildings with luxury apartments, high-end retail space, 311,176 square meters (3.35 million sf) of office space, and a world-class medical facility. The 564,000 square meters (6.07 million sf) of floor area is concentrated in one quadrant of the site, leaving over 40 percent of the project area reserved for an expansive, urban park that links to the community greenbelt.

The project area has housed a variety of former uses: a Japanese army garrison, residences for the post–World War II occupation forces, and most recently, the headquarters of Japan's Defense Agency.

DEVELOPMENT TEAM

Owner/Developer
Mitsui Fudosan Group
Tokyo, Japan
www.mitsuifudosan.co.jp

Master Architect
Skidmore, Owings & Merrill, LLP
New York, New York
www.som.com

Architect of Record
Nikken Sekkei Ltd
Tokyo, Japan
www.nikken.co.jp

Landscape Architect
EDAW
San Francisco, California
www.edaw.com

Associate Architects
Tadao Ando Architects & Associates
Osaka, Japan

Jun Aoki & Associates
Tokyo, Japan
www.aokijun.com

Communication Arts, Inc.
Boulder, Colorado
www.commarts-boulder.com

Kengo Kuma & Associates
Tokyo, Japan
www.kkaa.co.jp

Sakakura Associates
Tokyo, Japan
www.sakakura.co.jp

JURY STATEMENT

Tokyo Midtown represents a strategy by one developer to shift public perception of the Roppongi district from its reputation as a nighttime destination to an updated view—one that makes the area as vital during the day as it is at night. The mixed-use development is integrated with, and doubles the area of, a public park to create an environmentally sensitive and commercially active attraction that serves the entire neighborhood and adds economic value to nearby properties.

When the ministry relocated from Roppongi, it opened a continuous urban site for development in a city center where available land is scarce.

The Roppongi area has long been considered a "night town" favored by expatriates, better known as a free-wheeling entertainment hub than as a traditional neighborhood. Recent mixed-use developments in the area have begun to change that perception, and Tokyo Midtown aspires to permanently transform the district's image into a balanced mix of businesses and homes, with an emphasis on cultural amenities. In fact, the relocation of the famed Suntory Museum of Art to the site completes the Roppongi "art triangle," with the nearby Tokyo National Art Center and Roppongi Hills Mori Arts Center.

In 2001, when developer Mitsui Fudosan began the project, Japan was in a recession. The development team envisioned Tokyo Midtown as an emblem of a resurgent Japanese economy and sought to collect the best characteristics of Japanese society and display them in a single mixed-use development. The national government designated the Roppongi area as a "priority urban redevelopment area," which positioned the project to receive subsidies of approximately ¥2 billion (US$18.5 million) over four years for public improvements. The grant was applied to the construction of an underground passageway 470 meters (1,542 ft) long, which links the site to the neighborhood subway station.

The master plans were created collaboratively among the developer; Skidmore, Owings & Merrill as master architect; Nikken Sekkei as the project architect; and EDAW as the master landscape architect. The design team achieved a harmonious balance between dense, vertical development and ample outdoor areas by clustering all the buildings on the southeast portion of the site. Doing so reserved four continuous hectares (9.9 ac) of green space—or over 40 percent of the project area—which was bolstered by the integration and refinement of an adjacent public park. The project's large community park also links to an existing greenbelt that connects the project area to abundant neighboring green space, including the grounds of a Tokyo government cemetery and a Shinto religious shrine. Rather than raze the entire site, the design team carefully removed and transplanted 140 mature cherry and camphor trees located on the original Defense Agency grounds.

PROJECT DATA

Website
www.tokyo-midtown.com

Site Area
6.9 ha (17 ac)

Facilities
311,176 m² (3.35 million sf) office
70,993 m² (764,162 sf) retail
517 multifamily units
248 hotel rooms
1,226 parking spaces

Land Uses
office, retail, restaurant, hotel,
   entertainment, museum, medical,
   parks/open space

Start/Completion Dates
February 2004–March 2007

At a height of 248 meters (814 ft), Midtown Tower—the second-tallest building in Tokyo—soars from the center of the building podium. The Ritz-Carlton Tokyo occupies the top nine and bottom three floors of the skyscraper and includes 248 guest rooms. Two smaller towers for the Konami corporation and Fuji Film stand at the base of the Midtown Tower, in a formation inspired by a traditional Japanese rock garden.

The Galleria, an expansive four-story shopping arcade, is the main retail center at Tokyo Midtown. The enclosed space, 150 meters (492 ft) long and 25 meters (82 ft) high, features more than 130 stores, including a 24-hour high-end grocery. More than 517 multifamily units are housed in a single tower with a landscaped roof, and the project includes a world-class medical facility for the community—a product of an international partnership with Johns Hopkins Medicine International.

Tokyo Midtown features a number of environmentally friendly designs: landscaped building roofs minimize stormwater runoff, photovoltaic arrays provide a renewable energy source, recycled rainwater is used for landscaping, sodium-sulfur batteries store late-night electricity to stabilize power use at peak demand, and the building façades use sunlight-triggered window blinds. The project introduces a regional heating and cooling system to the district, which includes the recovery of waste heat created during gas-fired power generation. The vast green space not only provides recreational opportunities for residents and workers, but also reduces the heat island effect associated with most concrete-laden urban developments. A postconstruction survey revealed the surface temperature is three degrees Celsius (5.4 degrees F) lower than surrounding areas during the summer.

Tokyo Midtown has become a new center of activity in the Roppongi neighborhood, with 28 million people visiting in the first nine months. Retailers are expected to post ¥30 billion (US$278 million) in annual sales; the initial forecast was ¥25 billion (US$232 million). The public approval process and construction time frame took less time than anticipated, allowing the project to open a year ahead of schedule. The early opening led to additional rental revenues of approximately ¥30 billion (US$278 million) in the project's first year.

SITE PLAN

N

AKASAKA JUNIOR
HIGH SCHOOL

40 x 40 m
HELICOPTER
ZONE

HINOKICHO
PARK

MINATO-KU RD.

BLDG 'C'

BLDG 'A'

BLDG 'D'

BLDG 'E'

BLDG 'B'

GAIEN HIGASHI ST.

Avalon Chrystie Place/ Bowery Place

NEW YORK CITY, NEW YORK

The Avalon Chrystie Place/Bowery Place project is a four-phase, mixed-use development in the once-blighted Bowery neighborhood on the Lower East Side. Located on four separate sites—the majority of which have stood vacant for 50 years—the mixed-income project includes 120,000 square feet (11,148 m^2) of retail development; 699 apartment homes, 174 of which are reserved for low-income families; and a 42,700-square-foot (3,967-m^2) community center. The enormously complex project overcame a litany of obstacles, including political gridlock, unforeseen engineering challenges, and a multilayered financing scheme, and now stands as a catalyst in the emerging neighborhood.

The Lower East Side sites were developed early in Manhattan's history, with the Bowery becoming one of the borough's most elegant streets by the early 1800s. By the turn of the 20th century, however,

DEVELOPMENT TEAM

Owners/Developers
AvalonBay Communities, Inc.
Alexandria, Virginia
www.avaloncommunities.com

The Phipps Houses Group
New York, New York
www.phippsny.org

Design Architect
Arquitectonica
New York, New York
www.arquitectonica.com

Architect of Record
SLCE Architects
New York, New York
www.slcearch.com

the area had descended into extraordinary decay, with brothels and flophouses replacing the street's elegant mansions and storefronts. Overshadowed by the Third Avenue elevated train, the neighborhood suffered from high crime and disinvestment throughout the 20th century.

In 2002, New York City issued a request for proposals for the 3.2-acre (1.3-ha) site. Indicative of the long process ahead, the city was able to move forward with the request only after a multiyear community outreach effort built consensus on the redevelopment. The Cooper Square Task Force, the advisory committee charged with overseeing the project, issued strict conditions for the project: density and height were limited to preserve the human scale of the neighborhood; 25 percent of the apartments were to be reserved as affordable units; the community garden was to remain; and the development must include a core and shell for a new community center. In the end, the city selected AvalonBay's proposal, and the developer acquired the land for $41 million.

Designed by Arquitectonica, the master plan calls for the four new buildings to respond to the scale and character of the surrounding neighborhood, rather than appear as a monolithic project. The first phase, the 14-story Chrystie building, includes 361 apartment homes, 72 of which are affordable. The largest of the four structures, Chrystie Place effectively functions as three separate buildings: the residential component along Chrystie Street; a two-story, 72,000-square-foot (6,689-m²) Whole Foods—the largest grocery store in Manhattan; and the state-of-the-art community center on the

Bowery, which includes a basketball court and a six-lane swimming pool. The construction required an innovative engineering solution to build atop the 6th Avenue cross-town subway tunnel, which was installed just a few feet below the surface. The building's basement was built around the subway tunnel, and the community center pool—designed originally to go underground—now sits atop the basketball court, girded by a steel structure.

The second and third buildings, Avalon Bowery Place I and II, consist of 296 apartments in studio, one-bedroom, and two-bedroom configurations and will feature nine turnkey retail spaces, ranging from 1,200 square feet (111 m²) to 6,900 square feet (641 m²), each targeted toward local merchants and restaurateurs.

The construction of Bowery Place had to address the adjacent Liz Chrystie Community Garden. Founded in 1973, the community garden was the first in New York City and is the subject of fierce neighborhood protection. The design of Bowery Place was adjusted to preserve existing trees, and the developer created a $50,000 plant replacement fund to protect against the loss of any trees during construction.

The fourth building was developed by Phipps House, the city's oldest and largest developer of affordable housing. To achieve the 25 percent affordable housing mandate, all 42 units at the Extra Place Apartments are reserved for qualifying low-income families, which allowed the other three buildings to be developed at the traditional 80/20 ratio of market-rate to affordable housing.

Where many redevelopment efforts of the Bowery had failed—since the area was designated as an urban renewal district in 1959, opposition groups have outlasted five mayors and endless proposals—AvalonBay's plan proved to be a resounding success. All 699 apartments are currently occupied, with the market-rate component fetching some of the highest rents in the country: monthly one-bedroom rents average $4,000, with two-bedroom units commanding well over $5,500. AvalonBay speculates that based on recent sales of similar apartment buildings in Manhattan, the complex would be worth $568 million, creating a net value of $260 million.

PROJECT DATA

Websites
www.avaloncommunities.com/
  avaloncore/nfloor
www.avalonboweryplace.com

Site Area
3.2 ac (1.3 ha)

Facilities
116,000 sf (10,777 m²) retail/
  restaurant/entertainment space
699 multifamily units
181 underground parking spaces

Land Uses
residential, retail, restaurant,
  entertainment, civic, structured
  parking, open space

Start/Completion Dates
October 2003–November 2007

PHOTOGRAPHS BY M. OHREM-LECLEF, NYC

Church Street Plaza

EVANSTON, ILLINOIS

A product of a public/private endeavor among Arthur Hill & Co., the city of Evanston, and Northwestern University, Church Street Plaza is a $181 million mixed-use development around transit with 174,000 gross leasable square feet (16,165 m²) of retail, restaurant, and entertainment space. Considered the catalyst for downtown Evanston's decade-long resurgence, Church Street Plaza took advantage of a creative financing and partnership model to revitalize the urban core. The 7.2-acre (2.9-ha) project serves as a gateway between downtown Evanston and Northwestern University and also includes an 18-screen cinema, a 178-room hotel, a 204-unit condominium building, a 195,000-square-foot (59,436-m²) office building, and a 1,400-car parking garage.

Evanston, a first-ring suburb of Chicago, has seen its retail base decline steadily over the decades: once a regional shopping destination, by the 1980s, the city had not a single department store left within its limits. Determined to counteract the erosion of its commercial tax base, the city decided to encourage dense, mixed-use development through a variety of regulatory tools and incentives rather than focus on the traditional economic development strategy of attracting individual retailers. Church Street Plaza stands as the central component of the city of Evanston's strategic plan for the redevelopment of downtown.

The triangular site, a former surface parking lot, was situated in a non-tax-generating area at the intersection of two rail lines, effectively dividing the east and west sides of downtown. The tract included land owned by both the city of Evanston and Northwestern University—each of whom had conflicting opinions on how to redevelop the property. To overcome this obstacle, local developer Arthur Hill & Co. floated a proposal for the site in 1996 that focused on addressing the shopping and entertainment needs of both residents and students. Intrigued, the city of Evanston used the idea to sponsor an open developer-architect competition to produce a master plan for the site. In 1998, after a lengthy selection process, the team of Arthur Hill & Co. and ELS Architecture and Urban Design was selected based on its zero-lot-line master plan that used the entire tract and reinforced the existing street pattern.

To assuage the city's concern that a mixed-use district developed by a single entity would result in monotonous, uninspired architecture, four design firms provided their resources and signature touches to various buildings within the design criteria of the master plan. "This approach assured that the development looked more like a piece of the downtown urban fabric constructed as cities are, over time, rather than as a single project," explains Arthur Hill, chairman of Arthur Hill & Co.

During the selection process, the local business community raised the issue of how the large-scale project would affect the already challenged stores in downtown Evanston. The new mixed-use complex has proven to be a regional magnet, however; local officials estimate the project is responsible for over $200 million in additional residential and commercial development in Evanston's central busi-

DEVELOPMENT TEAM

Master Developer/Owner
Arthur Hill & Co., LLC
Evanston, Illinois
www.ahcrealty.com

Owners
Hilton Hotel
Beverly Hills, California
www.hiltonworldwide.com

Optima, Inc.
Glencoe, Illinois
www.optimaweb.com

Oppenheim Immobilien-
  Kapitalanlagegesellschaft
Köln, Germany
www.oppenheim.de

Developers
Regent Partners, Inc.
Atlanta, Georgia
www.regentpartners.com

Mesirow Stein Real Estate, Inc.
Chicago, Illinois
www.mesirowfinancial.com

Master Planner/Design Architect
ELS Architecture and Urban Design
Berkeley, California
www.elsarch.com

Architect of Record
DeStefano + Partners
Chicago, Illinois
www.destefanoandpartners.com

ness district. Downtown Evanston now has more than 80 new restaurants and 1,000 new residential units, providing a critical density that encourages even more retailers to flock to the city.

By any measure, Church Street Plaza has been a financial success: Century Theatres, the main entertainment anchor, reports its Evanston complex is a solidly profitable location; the condominium project is 100 percent sold; the Hilton hotel enjoys 80 percent occupancy and outpaces its regional competitors; the office building attracted a major tenant and is 99 percent leased; and the turnkey parking garage is generating $1.3 million in revenue for the city annually. Increased property and sales taxes further benefit the city, while the service-oriented hotel has provided much-needed lodging options for visitors to Northwestern University.

SITE PLAN

UNIVERSITY PLACE

7   7

8

MAPLE AVENUE

3

7

2

CLARK STREET

BENSON STREET

5

1

6

PROGRAM:

1. Retail / Entertainment Pavilion
2. Public Garage
3. Hotel
4. Office / Retail Building
5. Residential Condominium
6. Retail (Borders)

DOWNTOWN EXISTING USES

7. Northwestern University
8. Saturday Farmer's Market
9. Metra Rail
10. CTA Rail

CHURCH STREET

4

9

10

SCALE: 25' 50'   100'   200'

N

DAVIS STREET

Corvinus University Campus

BUDAPEST, HUNGARY

At first glance, the Corvinus University/Studium office building is merely another seven-story office block—albeit a Class A office building with a spectacular vista of the Danube and a multitude of amenities—in downtown Budapest. But the story of how this development came to be is a first in Hungary, a country that shifted in 1989 from a centrally planned economy to a free-market system and one still unaccustomed to public/private partnerships. The Corvinus University/Studium building is a win-win-win achievement for a public university (Corvinus), a private developer (Wing), and the city of Budapest.

A state-run institution, Corvinus University of Budapest was established in 2000 with the merger of two predecessor institutions—one that granted degrees in public administration, and another for economics and business administration—founded in the early years of the 20th century. A third faculty, horticulture and food sciences, joined in 2003. The next monumental step for the university came in 2004, with Hungary's acceptance in the European Union (EU).

DEVELOPMENT TEAM

Owner/Developer
Wing Zrt.
Budapest, Hungary
www.wallisrealestate.hu

Public Partner
Corvinus University of Budapest
Budapest, Hungary
www.uni-corvinus.hu

Architect of Record
Konstruma Kft.
Budapest, Hungary
www.konstruma.hu

Design Architects
AD Studio
Budapest, Hungary

Wing Design
Budapest, Hungary

Suddenly, Hungary's industries were expected to meet pan-European standards for all aspects of the economy—from educational quality and accreditation to electronic specifications, from agricultural output to communications compatibility. Corvinus University, along with all state institutions in Hungary, was presented with a mandate to modernize, improve, and compete. One part of Corvinus's response was to add a new academic and administrative building.

Housed in three urban campuses, Corvinus occupied the same facilities as the three original separate institutions that formed it. The faculties of business administration, economics, and social sciences, along with the main library and central administrative offices of the university, were housed in a 9,500-square-meter (102,257-sf) neoclassical palazzo from the late 1800s.

As Corvinus grew (its current enrollment is about 10,000 full-time and 7,000 part-time undergraduate and graduate students, and its seven faculties number 867), additional academic space was needed. For this purpose, the city transferred a 0.72-hectare (1.8-ac) parcel on the next block to Corvinus, but it remained undeveloped for several years because of a lack of capital, experience, and capacity.

When the need for additional facilities became overwhelming, especially after Hungary joined the EU, the state began a yearlong public bidding process to find the right development partner. Wing Zrt., the development arm of the Hungarian conglomerate Wallis Group, was chosen in 2005 for its innovative proposal and for its experience in successfully managing public projects. Wing proposed to lease back the parcel from the state for an indefinite period while owning the building and leasing 24,000 square meters (258,334 sf) of academic space to the university for 20 years at dramatically below-market rates. Wing would rent out the remaining 12,000 square meters (129,167 sf) and collect additional income from two levels of underground parking.

Essentially a turnkey development, the project was delivered in an unheard-of 27 months between site acquisition and move-in. Because of the site's location just outside the boundaries of a UNESCO World Heritage precinct that governs construction on the Danube embankment, the university required that the architectural design be compatible with the historic neighborhood. The 135-by-65-

meter (443-by-213-ft) trapezoidal city block was cleared of buildings, except for a historic building on a 1,600-square-meter (17,222-sf) corner of the block. On the remaining 7,200 square meters (77,500 sf), the developer built a seven-story complex with two interior courtyards. Two underground parking levels have entry/exit points at the two side streets. At ground level are retail spaces, part of which is occupied by a restaurant.

The Corvinus University component accommodates nearly 3,500 students and 300 faculty and staff in 32 classrooms, 19 seminar rooms, six lecture halls, a 500-seat auditorium-seating lecture hall, and a 100,000-volume library. The Studium office component faces the city-owned open space between the project and the Danube. This back-to-back configuration helps reduce the cross-traffic between the active urban university and the more sedate Class A office, and it gives the office component an unobstructed view of the Danube from street level to penthouse.

The building's location, within two blocks of the soon-to-open Metro 4 subway station, and its shared site with a university whose intellectual resources are applicable to businesses were a prime attraction for Nokia, the cell-phone manufacturer, which occupies 95 percent of the leasable office space as its Hungarian headquarters. Wing's return on the project's €43.8 million (US$63.9 million) cost (on a land lease) is currently 8.7 percent, scheduled to rise to 9.72 percent when income is fully stabilized, which compares to an average of 5.0 to 6.5 percent for similar developments in Budapest.

PROJECT DATA

Website
www.studiumofficebuilding.hu
www.uni-corvinus.hu

Site Area
0.72 ha (1.8 ac)

Facilities
2,400 m² (25,833 sf) academic and
   university space
1,200 m² (12,917 sf) office space
210 m m² (2,260 sf) retail and
   restaurant space
408 parking spaces

Land Uses
education, office, retail, restaurant,
   parking, open space

Start/Completion Dates
June 2005–September 2007

Liberty Hotel/ Yawkey Center

BOSTON, MASSACHUSETTS

The Liberty Hotel/Yawkey Center project seamlessly blends two uses not commonly associated with each other—a hotel and hospital—on a three-acre (1.2-ha) shared site. In addition to the unconventional partnering, the development includes an adaptive use of the Charles Street Jail, a historic landmark at the northern base of Boston's Beacon Hill neighborhood. Ultimately, a common planning vision between the developer and the owner united the disparate functions, resulting in a $150 million, 300-room luxury hotel and 440,000-square-foot (40,877-m²) state-of-the-art outpatient facility.

In 1991, Massachusetts General Hospital acquired the Charles Street Jail site from the commonwealth after federal courts found the jail building unfit for prisoners and ordered it decommissioned. Located directly adjacent to the hospital's main campus, the prison site afforded the hospital's direc-

DEVELOPMENT TEAM

Owners/Developers
Carpenter & Company, Inc.
Cambridge, Massachusetts
www.carpenterandcompanyinc.com

Kennedy Associates Real Estate
  Counsel LP
Seattle, Washington
www.kennedyusa.com

Owner
Massachusetts General Hospital
Boston, Massachusetts
www.massgeneral.org

Architect
Cambridge Seven Associates, Inc.
Cambridge, Massachusetts
www.c7a.com

Historic Preservation Architect
Ann Beha Associates
Boston, Massachusetts
www.annbeha.com

115

PROJECT DATA

Website
www.libertyhotel.com
www.massgeneral.org

Site Area
3 ac (1.2 ha)

Facilities
440,000 sf (40,877 m²) medical
230,000 sf (21,368 m²) hotel
298 hotel rooms
700 underground parking spaces

Land Uses
medical, hotel, restaurant,
  structured parking, open space

Start/Completion Dates
2001–2007

tors an opportunity to accommodate the medical facility's expanding operations. By the late 1990s, the developer had identified two potential uses for the site: first, as a state-of-the-art outpatient care facility, or second, as a high-quality hotel for visitors and families of patients. When the 157-year-old jail quickly proved unsuitable for a modern hospital facility, the developer discovered both uses could be realized through careful planning of a shared site.

The key to the design concept was the historic Charles Street Jail. The imposing structure—which once imprisoned Sacco and Vanzetti—was completed in 1851 and stands as one of the foremost examples of the Boston Granite style of architecture. Listed on the state and national Registers of Historic Places, the jail was constructed in the shape of a cross, with four wings extending from an octagonal rotunda at the center. In contrast to the windowless, bleak penitentiaries of today, the historic prison reflected the most progressive approaches to jail design at the time: for example, 30 arched windows—each 30 feet (9.1 m) in height—allow plentiful natural light and ventilation.

The redevelopment of the historic prison, undertaken by Carpenter & Company and buttressed by the sale of state and federal tax credits, included a meticulous renovation of the central atrium, which rises 90 feet (27.4 m) high. Now serving as the hotel's lobby, the expansive, three-level space's exposed, trussed ceiling was painstakingly restored, and the trademark catwalks that surround the chamber were retained and widened. Ultimately, the cost premium associated with the rehabilitation of the prison building was in excess of $15 million.

The plan, designed by Cambridge Seven Associates, reused three wings and the original atrium of the Charles Street Jail as the public spaces—lobby, restaurants, and conference rooms—of the Liberty

Hotel, while the fourth, eastern wing links to the new Yawkey Center. The majority of the hotel's rooms are located in a newly constructed, 15-story building to the north of the jail, while the modern outpatient facility replaced a five-story parking structure to the east. The two facilities share 700 below-grade parking spaces, along with a landscaped outdoor plaza.

The construction of the Liberty Hotel/Yawkey Center project faced a number of technical challenges: a constrained building site, highly sensitive hospital uses nearby, and historic preservation delays. Bounded on three sides by important hospital facilities or heritage buildings, the construction of the Yawkey Center used an "up-down" model that allowed the surrounding uses to remain operational and condensed the construction window to less than three years. Self-imposed restrictions on construction vibration and hours of operation at the project site allowed the adjacent Proton Therapy Center—a high-tech radiation facility dependent on carefully calibrated equipment—to remain open throughout the development process. Because of the sensitive nature of historic rehabilitation, the preservation requirements lengthened the preconstruction phase; however, the associated tax credits represented a considerable savings on the project.

Both the Liberty Hotel and Yawkey Center have been highly successful since their completion in 2007. In its first few months of operation, the Liberty Hotel has provided high-quality accommodations in an area formerly bereft of hotel rooms, and the project's bars and restaurants have opened to critical acclaim. The hospital's new outpatient facility has already exceeded the projected five-year patient volume, just three years after opening, and has extended its operating hours to meet demand.

PHOTOGRAPHS BY BRUCE MARTIN (114, 115R); ANTON GRASSL (115L); KWESI ARTHUR (116); CARPENTER & COMPANY, INC.; MASSACHUSETTS GENERAL HOSPITAL (117L); PETER VANDERWARKER (117R)

Life Hub @ Daning

SHANGHAI, CHINA

A modern version of a traditional Chinese commercial hub, Life Hub @ Daning has transformed one of Shanghai's most underserved urban districts—the fast-growing, formerly industrial neighborhood of Zhabei in northern Shanghai—into a trendy commercial zone with extensive entertainment and cultural offerings. The project targets the rapidly growing middle class of Shanghai and has ambitions of becoming a regional shopping center, as evidenced by the numbers of visitors from beyond the city limits. It serves the neighborhood's more than 1 million residents as well as shoppers within a 20-kilometer (12-mi) radius.

With 15 buildings and 250,000 square meters (2.7 million sf) of space, the 5.5-hectare (13.6-ac) development includes a 326-room Four Points by Sheraton hotel; 38,000 square meters (409,029 sf) of office space in four buildings set atop retail podiums; 50,000 square meters (538,196 sf) of retail space; 48,000 square meters (516,668 sf) of food and entertainment offerings; 12,000 square meters (129,167 sf) of cultural and service facilities; and 1,300 parking spaces above and below ground. Life Hub was developed by Shanghai Forrester (Zhabei) Development Ltd., a subsidiary of the Chongbang Group.

"Life Hub @ Daning has created a new benchmark for Shanghai's urban development and a new lifestyle for the city's residents and visitors," says Henry Cheng, director and chief executive officer of the Chongbang Group. "Its multiple functions, its unique ambience, its quality tenants, its large scale, its proactive property and operational management team, and its ever growing popularity among consumers have greatly enhanced the land value and living standard of a relatively underdeveloped district in urban Shanghai."

When Shanghai Forrester first conceived the project in late 2003, population growth in the area was imminent, but increased market demand was not yet apparent. The developer's bold decision to build a massive project in a single phase has enabled it to capture a broad market base and create a strong market presence. The developer established a fast-track construction process that aimed to complete the CNY 1.9 billion (US$250 million) project within the then-current government's term in office, effectively securing support from government officials to expedite the approval process.

Designed by RTKL Dallas, Life Hub's open-plan concept incorporates 11 interconnected courtyards and piazzas as well as approximately two kilometers (1.2 mi) of landscaped pedestrian promenades, creating a more leisurely environment than the hustle and bustle seen in downtown Shanghai. Modern high-, mid-, and low-rise structures, built and arranged in the scale and proportion of a traditional Chinese commercial center, present a new yet familiar cityscape.

The project, located between two subway stations, attracts more than 60,000 visitors per day on weekdays and more than 100,000 per day on weekends. Positioned as a signature destination for Shanghai's young and fast-growing middle class through its merchandise mix, pricing, advertising, and promotions, Life Hub rewards returning customers through bar-coded membership cards with

DEVELOPMENT TEAM

Owners/Developers
Shanghai Forrester (Zhabei)
  Development Ltd.
Shanghai, China
www.daningdaning.com

Chongbang Holdings Limited
Shanghai, China
www.daningdaning.com

Architect
RTKL Associates, Inc.
Dallas, Texas
www.rtkl.com

which they can access the latest information about the center using their cell phones, the first program of this kind in Shanghai.

The office component was sold to a global financial institution, and Chongbang Holdings is retaining the rest of the property. It expects the return on its investment to exceed 16 percent when the project's income stream has stabilized, targeted for mid-2008. Life Hub has created value for the surrounding area as well. The average selling price for residential units in the neighborhood, for example, has risen by more than 20 percent since the inception of the project, and a nearby development site recently sold for a record price. Life Hub has also been honored by the municipal government for providing the district with increased tax revenue and improving its image as a retail destination.

Life Hub is a leadership model for the professional development of commercial properties serving the burgeoning middle class in China. Over 80 percent of the tenants are newcomers to the Daning district, providing a variety of goods and services previously unseen in the urban neighborhood. Life Hub's increased accessibility, new retail typology, and cultural programming all have set new benchmarks.

PHOTOGRAPHS BY SHANGHAI FORRESTER (ZHABEI) DEVELOPMENT LTD

Lincoln Square

BELLEVUE, WASHINGTON

Derailed by the 2001 dot-com bust, the Lincoln Square project, an ambitious mixed-use development in the Seattle suburb of Bellevue, left a considerable hole in the downtown market—quite literally in the form of a five-story, abandoned construction pit. With office vacancies in the city soaring from 5 percent to 28 percent in two years and a city-ordained requirement that all components be built simultaneously, the original developer was forced to halt construction in the summer of 2002, leaving only the half-complete underground parking and foundation for an office building. The high-tech decline hit the city of Bellevue especially hard, as expanding Internet startups in the region gave the illusion of demand for downtown office space. The construction site lay fallow for over a year as the out-of-town developer shopped the project around, leaving the community with an eyesore in the heart of the city.

In August 2003, Kemper Development Company (KDC), owner of the successful, adjacent Bellevue Square and Bellevue Center retail projects, took on the challenge of turning around the Lincoln Square project—a massive risk in the uncertain economic climate of the early 2000s. After four years of redesign and innovative construction, the 1.4 million-square-foot (130,064 m²) mixed-use project, replete with 300,000 square feet (2,787 m²) of retail; a 28-story, Class A office tower; 148 luxury condominiums; and a 19-story hotel, has resuscitated a moribund development and brought much-needed density to a suburban environment. The two towers rise from five stories of underground parking and a three-level retail podium, featuring a luxury cinema, restaurants, home-related stores, and upscale entertainment.

The locally based developer acquired the property for $40 million, taking the troubled project off the hands of the original owner, who had already sunk $215 million into the development. KDC did possess a few built-in advantages for this potentially hazardous undertaking: decades of working with Bellevue officials had fostered goodwill, expediting the entitlement process; also, the developer's adjacent retail magnets allowed complementary design, tenants, and amenities.

Before KDC commenced construction, the design team—led by Sclater Partners—overhauled the site plan to make the retail component more marketable and successful. The major redesign focused on transforming the retail podium from an inward-facing, anchorless series of small shops to a street-level, retail, restaurant, and entertainment scheme. The city of Bellevue is characterized by 1950s-style superblocks 600 feet (183 m) long and six-lane-wide arterials that limit ground-floor retail options. The Lincoln Square project establishes a street-level presence—a rare sight in the suburban enclave—in hopes of fostering the nascent urbanism of downtown Bellevue.

The design team connected the project to the adjacent shopping malls, Bellevue Square and Bellevue Place, with two skybridges and a pedestrian tunnel, linking Lincoln Square to two of the most successful retail complexes in the Pacific Northwest. The sleek glass-and-steel walkways—suspended

DEVELOPMENT TEAM

Owner/Developer
Kemper Development Company
Bellevue, Washington

Architect
Sclater Partners Architects
Seattle, Washington
www.sclaterpartners.com

by tensile cables—provide much-needed foot traffic to the second and third levels of the Lincoln Square atrium that is ringed with restaurants and shops. KDC attracted tenants that would complement, rather than compete with, its sister developments, targeting, for instance, larger-format, home-related retailers that were absent from KDC's other projects.

The mixed-use project presented a number of challenges, most notably in the construction of the office tower. With the retail podium already open, the general contractor was given the daunting job of building over the busiest intersection in the region without disturbing tenants and the improved streetscape below. To meet this challenge, the construction team created a unique structural platform: built atop the retail podium and shielded from view below, the construction stage could be moved upward with each floor added to the office building.

Part of KDC's decade-long effort to bring a vibrant, dense mix of uses to the outer suburb of Bellevue, the success of Lincoln Square has also positioned the city as a competitive retail destination in the Pacific Northwest. The calculated risk of redeveloping the failed site has paid off: the office component—the pitfall of the original project—was 100 percent leased above market rates before ground was broken; the shopping mall has experienced record-setting sales and traffic figures; the luxury hotel continues to perform at high levels in occupancy and rate; and the Lincoln Square Cinemas has been a top national performer in blockbuster openings.

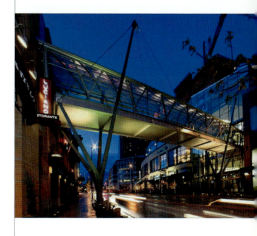

PROJECT DATA

Website
www.lincolnsquare.com

Site Area
32.1 ac (13 ha)

Facilities
540,000 sf (50,168 m²) office
300,000 sf (27,871 m²) retail
148 multifamily units
337 hotel rooms
1,700 underground parking

Land Uses
office, residential, retail, restaurant,
  hotel, parking

Start/Completion Dates
February 2004–July 2007

South Campus Gateway

COLUMBUS, OHIO

South Campus Gateway is a visionary collaboration between the Ohio State University, the city of Columbus, and neighborhood stakeholders in an effort to transform a 7.5-acre (three-ha) tract that straddles the university campus and a distressed, low-income neighborhood. Developed by the not-for-profit Campus Partners, the $150 million dynamic mixed-use development is the signature project in the organization's decade-long planning effort to revitalize the University District area. Using a complex layering of financing, the project comprises 184 apartments, 98,000 square feet (9,105 m²) of office space, and 249,000 square feet (23,133 m²) of retail stores, including an eight-screen cinema, a dozen restaurants, a university bookstore, and an organic grocery.

In the early 1990s, Ohio State began to take note of High Street, the troubled main thoroughfare that runs along the eastern border of campus. In particular, the university focused on a two-mile (3.2-km) stretch of low-slung bars and abandoned properties that were marred by blight and disinvestment. In 1995, Ohio State formed Campus Partners, a not-for-profit agency with a 15-member governing board that includes the city's development director, several neighborhood activists, and student representation, to study alternatives for the area.

DEVELOPMENT TEAM

Owner/Developer
Campus Partners
Columbus, Ohio
www.campuspartners.osu.edu

Architect
Elkus Manfredi Architects
Boston, Massachusetts
www.elkus-manfredi.com

Master Planner
Goody Clancy
Boston, Massachusetts
www.goodyclancy.com

The multilayered financing for South Campus Gateway was patched together from various institutional and public sources. The $20 million, four-year assembly of 31 separate parcels—achieved by negotiated relocations and eminent domain—was financed through Ohio State's Endowment Fund. The city of Columbus provided $8 million for public improvements, including burial of overhead utility lines, relocation of storm and sanitary sewers, roadway improvements, and sidewalk construction. The portions of the South Campus Gateway developed for the university's public use were financed through the sale of tax-exempt bonds, generating an additional $110 million. For the private-use, retail component, Campus Partners received $35 million in tax credits under the New Markets Tax Credit program—the largest such allocation for a single project in the country.

Using city and university funds, Boston-based urban planners Goody Clancy created the master plan that would govern the development of the three-block section of High Street. The intention was to repair the seam between the university and the local neighborhood by activating the troubled corridor through a mix of commercial, residential, and entertainment uses.

A 50,000-square-foot (4,645-m²) University Bookstore anchors the corner of 11th Avenue and High Street; its five-level glass entrance opens toward campus and draws students into the heart of the project. The five-story street wall is maintained south along High Street through two apartment buildings and a 98,000-square-foot (9,105-m²) office structure, with the street-level experience animated by ground-floor retail establishments.

A pedestrian alley—lined with restaurants, bars, and an eight-screen cinema—bisects a large block, providing nightlife opportunities for students and residents. At its terminus sits a 1,200-space parking

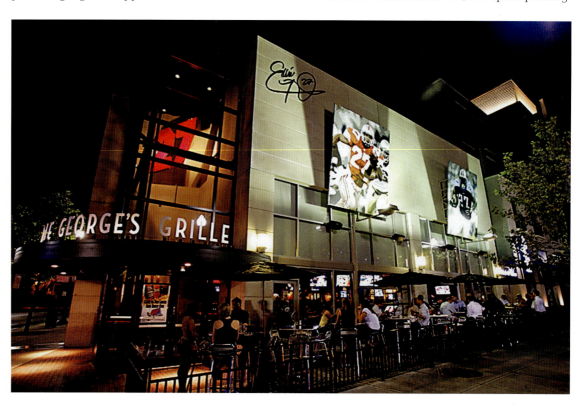

PHOTOGRAPHS BY THE PLAIN DEALER (126); BRAD FEINKNOPF (127); ELKUS MANFREDI ARCHITECTS (128L); ERIC WAGNER (128R); CAMPUS PARTNERS (129)

garage. The massive structure is situated at the interior of the site and is wrapped by three-story town-houses along the streetfront, reducing its perceived mass.

The buildings draw their architectural inspiration from the turn-of-the-century mercantile buildings found in Columbus's Short North neighborhood, but they are rendered with a contemporary aesthetic. The mix of uses provides 24-hour activity, creating an additional layer of security that has contributed to a significant decrease in crime in the neighboring community.

As a not-for-profit developer, Campus Partners considers more than just return on investment when measuring the success of a project. South Campus Gateway has positively affected the local community: more than 700 full-time jobs have been produced, with over half drawn from low-income communities; surrounding property values—once in free fall—have stabilized; students no longer have to drive off-campus for basic goods and services; and crime in the area has decreased markedly.

In economic terms, more than $30 million in private investment has been made along High Street and in adjacent residential neighborhoods in the University District since the project's inception. The South Campus Gateway has also established trust—an often-overlooked commodity—between neighboring communities and the university and can be used as a national model for urban universities seeking to spur redevelopment along their edges.

PROJECT DATA

Website
www.southcampusgateway.com

Site Area
7.5 ac (3 ha)

Facilities
98,000 sf (9,105 m²) office
249,000 sf (23,133 m²) retail
184 multifamily units
1,200 structured parking spaces

Land Uses
office, residential, retail, restaurant,
  entertainment, parking

Start/Completion Dates
2000–2005

RESIDENTIAL/PLANNED COMMUNITY

PHOTOGRAPHS BY CARLOS RODRIGUEZ (L); KIRINDA TRUST–COLLIERS INTERNATIONAL (LC); MIKE WERT, HOUSING AUTHORITY OF PORTLAND (LR); ART GRAY (R)

Army Residential Communities Initiative

UNITED STATES

In 1998, the U.S. Army faced a $7 billion funding deficit to upgrade substandard housing and build additional residential units at military bases around the country. Military family housing had descended to such an extreme state of disrepair that soldiers' morale was slumping, and recruiting and retention numbers were trending downward. Despite clear deficiencies in the hous-

DEVELOPMENT TEAM

Owner/Developer
Department of the Army
Arlington, Virginia
www.rci.army.mil

Real Estate Adviser
Jones Lang LaSalle
Chicago, Illinois
www.joneslanglasalle.com

JURY STATEMENT

Faced with a $7 billion funding deficit to upgrade substandard housing and to build new housing at military bases, the U.S. Army instituted the Residential Communities Initiative in 1998 to privatize housing on its bases. By leasing the land and conveying existing stock to private limited liability companies—which then become responsible for upgrades, new construction, management, and rent collection from the individual soldiers' housing allowances—the army has privatized 78,789 units at 36 bases with a 12:1 private-to-public funding ratio, enhancing the quality of life for soldiers and their families.

ing program, the Department of Defense neglected to allocate necessary funds from strained military budgets to make the critical improvements. Facing these challenges, the U.S. Army launched the Residential Communities Initiative (RCI) to privatize the renovation, construction, and operation of military housing.

At the time RCI was initiated, the army estimated that 70 percent of on-base family housing was inadequate—more than 88,000 units. Consequently, more than 10,000 families moved off post or were separated, as soldiers had to be housed separately from their spouses. With Jones Lang LaSalle as real estate adviser, the army's plan was to leverage private capital to renovate and construct military housing at little or no additional costs to taxpayers, thus enhancing soldiers' readiness, recruitment, and retention, despite the unfunded mandate.

RCI uses an innovative ownership and financial structure: the U.S. Army leases the property (for 50 years) to private sector limited liability companies (LLCs), conveying any existing housing, while retaining ultimate ownership of the land. The private sector partner operates the residential units, using the steady income stream from rents to obtain financing to make upgrades and build new units, thereby increasing long-term property value.

The RCI program faced two major obstacles: first, the wariness of the military establishment and legislators about privatizing public assets; and second, initial reluctance from traditional lenders to

finance an unproven program. Stakeholders at the Pentagon and Congress had initial doubts that a public/private partnership could be administered in a manner that expanded the army's housing inventory while maintaining long-term control over ownership—at one point, lawmakers delayed the program for a year. Jones Lang LaSalle and the army addressed every contingency, assuring the government that the program would comply with both military standards and federal regulations and that the land would remain a long-term public asset.

Initially, private financial sources were unwilling to invest in the untested RCI program. Without a source of debt financing for private sector partners to commit toward renovation and development projects—a critical component of the program—RCI could not move forward. To overcome this obstacle, RCI approached a nontraditional source of construction and acquisition financing: Wall Street. By creating investment vehicles that allowed different investors to buy varying tranches of risk with corresponding levels of return, RCI attracted the critical debt service for early-stage closings—albeit at a higher overall price. As the privatization program proved successful and the initial investors realized positive returns, banks and other institutional lenders, seeing that the risks were less than anticipated, began to approach acquisition and development firms with traditional financing options. This increased competition lowered the cost of capital for private sector partners.

Through the end of January 2008, the RCI program has transferred 78,789 homes at 36 army installations to the private sector, and in return, its partners have committed $10.5 billion to the renovation, demolition, and construction of new residences. The program has already produced noteworthy development types traditionally unseen in military housing: for example, a private sector partner developed the Village Commons at Fort Belvoir in northern Virginia, a mixed-use development with residential units above ground-floor retail space. Developed by Clark Pinnacle, the project is arranged around a pedestrian-oriented "Main Street," supplying army families with nearby shops and amenities, and a streetscape that fosters camaraderie—an important asset for the military market.

At the Kalakaua Community in Schofield, Hawaii, a private developer, Actus Lend Lease, has created a model for sustainable development on military bases. At buildout, the Kalakaua Community will consist of over 5,000 new Energy Star–certified homes and 2,500 rehabilitated residences powered by rooftop photovoltaic panels. Upon completion, it will be the largest solar-powered community in the United States. Motivated to meet the U.S. Army's objective to decrease energy consumption 20 percent by 2010, the new urbanist community also features the SYNERGY (Saving Your Nation's Energy) program, which educates residents about energy consumption and efficiency methods.

RCI represents a dramatic, programmatic shift in how the military houses families in America. Today, the ratio of private-to-public funding is 12:1, relieving a fiduciary burden on the already-stressed budgets of the Department of Defense. The U.S. Army expects to realize a $7 billion cost savings when all inadequate housing is eliminated, and RCI is on schedule to meet its goals by 2016.

PROJECT DATA

Website
www.rci.army.mil

Site Area
36 military bases

Facilities
13,000 sf (1,208 m²) retail
78,789 single-family units (88,045 at buildout)
200 multifamily units (1,396 at buildout)
19,316 hotel rooms at buildout

Land Uses
residential, retail, office, civic, parks/open space

Start/Completion Dates
1999–2016

Eleven80

NEWARK, NEW JERSEY

The first new market-rate housing built in downtown Newark in more than 40 years, the 30-story Eleven80 building stands as a beacon, signaling the economic resurgence of a forgotten city. The luxury apartment building—converted from its original use as an office tower—consists of 316 units and features 8,000 square feet (743 m²) of retail space. It has been successfully luring tenants from the New York City market; over 80 percent of Eleven80's residents commute to Manhattan. Completed in 2006, the $120 million project was financed by seven separate private and public sources.

For 20 years, the classic structure had sat vacant, lapsing into deplorable conditions: years of water infiltration, freeze-thaw conditions, and mold and pest accumulation had caused almost irreparable

DEVELOPMENT TEAM

Owner/Developer
Cogswell Realty Group, LLC
Newark, New Jersey
www.cogswellrg.com

Architect
Gruzen Samton Architects LLP
New York, New York
www.gruzensamton.com

Historic Preservation Consultant
Building Conservation Associates, Inc.
New York, New York
www.bcausa.com

JURY STATEMENT

The first addition to downtown Newark's housing stock in over 40 years, Eleven80 restores a dilapidated—almost to the point of irreparability—75-year-old, 30-story office tower to a 316-unit condominium building with high-end amenities. Eleven80, along with the developer's adjacent National Newark Building, fulfills a part of the developer's vision for the city's revitalization—evidenced by Eleven80's attraction of former Manhattan residents.

damage to the edifice. Entire floor plates had rotted through, sections of the masonry façade were crumbling, and steel beams and columns had rusted and separated from the structure. By the turn of the 21st century, the presence of the deteriorating, vacant office tower in downtown Newark had become a constant reminder of the lack of economic progress in the once great city.

In 1998, Cogswell Realty Group, a privately owned New York real estate firm, purchased the 448-foot (137-m) art deco tower for $2.2 million. A pioneer in the field of urban redevelopment, Cogswell saw the potential of downtown Newark as an affordable residential alternative to New York City: Newark is only 20 minutes from Manhattan, with direct connections to the airport, the northeast corridor, and western suburbs via the local subway and rail stations. In addition, the Eleven80 site is adjacent to the six-acre (2.4-ha) Military Park and several downtown cultural and academic attractions, such as the New Jersey Performing Arts Center, the Newark Museum, and five downtown universities.

The primary challenge faced by the development team was acquiring the necessary financing to renovate the building. Cogswell Realty Group had to overcome the cynicism of traditional lenders—while the commercial market has gathered strength in Newark, obtaining credit for residential development has been substantially more difficult. The developer needed five years to cobble together $120 million from seven sources: traditional loans from a syndicate of three banks, the sale of federal historic preservation tax credits to Fannie Mae, various loans from state agencies, financing assistance from two private foundations that promote housing availability, and the developer's own equity investment to cover the remaining funding gap.

Cogswell hired the historic preservation firm Building Conservation Associates to painstakingly inventory and label all the historic elements of the building. Approximately 4,000 features had to be repaired on the building's façade alone; updated mechanical and electric equipment was helicoptered onto the roof; terra-cotta ornamentation was re-created; and all building infrastructure was replaced and updated for modern use.

Eleven80 contains 316 luxury rental units in studio, one-bedroom, and two-bedroom configurations with expansive, panoramic views from all four sides of the building. The apartment building offers high-end amenities, including an 8,000-square-foot (743-m²) health club, a private four-lane bowling alley, a cocktail lounge, an indoor basketball court, and valet parking. Rents are high by Newark standards—reaching $2,500 per month for a large two-bedroom unit—but are less than half of the prices commanded by comparable buildings in Manhattan and one-third less than those of closer-in Jersey City and Hoboken.

As it has infused market-rate housing into Newark's downtown, Eleven80 has affected the city's socioeconomic structure. Working with the Newark affirmative action office and the New Jersey Institute for Social Justice, Cogswell made a commitment to hire local community members to rehabilitate and construct the project and to have its union laborers train and qualify local residents for union apprenticeships. At the peak of construction, the project employed more than 400 local laborers and generated approximately $1.6 million in salaries for Newark residents.

Eleven80 opened its doors in August 2006, and rents are meeting, and in some cases exceeding, the pro forma projections. Cogswell Realty owns multiple properties near Eleven80 and hopes to develop ten more mixed-use projects, which would add another 3,000 residential units to the urban core. Beyond short-term economic gains, therefore, the success of Eleven80 may play a part in determining the future of downtown Newark.

PROJECT DATA

Website
www.Eleven80rentals.com

Site Area
0.3 ac (0.1 ha)

Facilities
8,000 sf (743 m²) retail
316 multifamily units

Land Uses
residential, retail

Start/Completion Dates
March 2005–December 2007

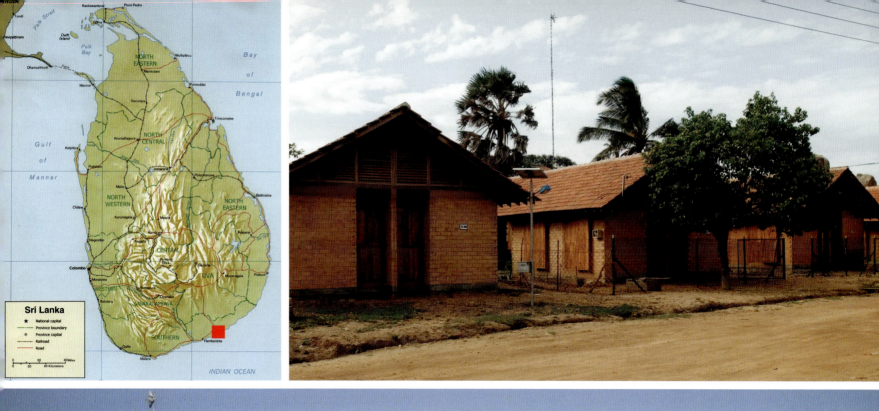

Kirinda Project

KIRINDA, SRI LANKA

In 2004, the small fishing village of Kirinda, located on the southeast tip of Sri Lanka, was ravaged by the great Asian tsunami that killed more than 225,000 people in 11 countries. The community was devastated: hundreds of villagers were killed or left homeless, and over 90 percent of the village's fishermen lost their livelihood in a single wave. After hearing of and viewing the effects of the tsunami, Philip Bay, the regional director of Colliers Southeast Europe, was compelled to act. Identifying Sri Lanka as one of the hardest-hit regions, Colliers International com-

DEVELOPMENT TEAM

Developer
Colliers Kirinda Trust
Athens, Greece
www.collierskirinda.com

Design Architect
Shigeru Ban Architects
Paris, France
www.shigerubanarchitects.com

JURY STATEMENT

The Kirinda Project is one real estate company's unique humanitarian and volunteer response to the devastation suffered by one fishing village in Sri Lanka in the aftermath of the great tsunami of 2004. Colliers pooled its and its clients' resources and expertise to expeditiously and effectively rebuild 50 homes, using traditional materials and methods to sensitively reestablish the village's cultural, social, and religious underpinnings.

menced discussions with the Sri Lankan government, offering to contribute its real estate expertise to the relief effort. Kirinda—one of the most thoroughly devastated communities of the island nation—was identified, and Colliers was asked to lead the reconstruction initiative.

Colliers International—a property company, not a nongovernmental organization (NGO)—used its expertise to finance and coordinate the effort to rebuild destroyed homes in Kirinda. The international real estate organization engaged Paris-based architect Shigeru Ban to create the town's first master plan, which governed the sustainable reconstruction of 50 single-family homes across the village's worst-hit area.

The organization approached the project and the village residents as clients, rather than as recipients of disaster relief. Many NGO relief organizations in Sri Lanka—although operating with the best intentions—hastily assembled concrete domiciles without input from the community or consideration of the culture and history of the inhabitants. In the worst cases, relief agencies squandered resources or skimmed donations, offering false hope to many devastated areas.

At Kirinda, a number of town-hall meetings with displaced inhabitants, local government officials,

147

and religious leaders informed and guided the master plan. The foremost desire of the local community was to restore the original village layout and its focal point: the mosque. Cognizant of avoiding community fragmentation—an unintentional byproduct of other rebuilding efforts in Sri Lanka—the project constructed the new houses on the exact plots of their destroyed predecessors. Furthermore, deeds and titles were drawn up for each of the inhabitants, allowing the villagers to engage more fully in the economy by using their homes as collateral for traditional loans.

Shigeru Ban, well known for his application of sustainable architecture in refugee and disaster areas elsewhere in the world, was selected to design the Kirinda project. Through research on the history of residential construction in Sri Lanka, Ban discovered little indigenous use of concrete on the island and much greater reliance on local resources, such as teak, rubber tree wood, and earthen materials. Nowadays, concrete is readily available and is the product of choice for most construction sites in Sri Lanka; however, the material retains heat—a severe disadvantage in Sri Lanka's sultry climate.

The design team reverted to traditional practice and used all local, sustainable products. The exterior walls of the houses were constructed with hand-pressed, sun-dried earthen blocks, made from a mix of sand and water, which allow the buildings to breathe in the stifling heat. Prefabricated interior wall units are made of teak purchased from a national tree farm. The simplicity of the exposed interior will make adaptation, expansion, and repair fairly straightforward, and the uniformity inherent in the design made construction very cost-effective. The use of local materials and labor also offered employment for the local people, most of whom had lost their livelihoods to the tsunami.

The Kirinda Project was funded entirely by money raised at Colliers' offices, including donations from employees and clients. To date, the trust has raised LKR 66.7 million (US$620,000), of which only 2 percent is consumed by administrative costs. The trust has only a single employee, the project coordinator based in Sri Lanka. The humanitarian effort relied on the skills of local architects, engineers, contractors, and project leaders to implement the master plan.

Colliers' Kirinda Project has become the benchmark by which other disaster relief organizations are measured. The Sri Lankan government routinely brings visiting delegations to Kirinda, using the reconstructed village as an example of best practice. Despite Colliers' complete lack of experience in disaster relief, Sri Lankan officials have publicly stated that the project was the most professionally executed tsunami-relief project in the country.

PROJECT DATA

Website
www.collierskirinda.com

Site Area
1.2 ha (3 ac)

Facilities
50 single-family units

Land Uses
residential

Start/Completion Dates
June 2005–February 2007

Solara

POWAY, CALIFORNIA

Developed by nonprofit Community HousingWorks (CHW) and located in the outer suburbs of San Diego, Solara is a green affordable community designed to be self-sufficiently powered through a photovoltaic system. The 2.5-acre (one-ha) project includes a number of other sustainable and green building features, such as passive solar design, low-maintenance landscaping, and the use of recycled materials throughout the site. A pioneer in the use of renewable energy at multifamily projects, CHW used a creative mix of state and federal incentives to finance the 56-unit complex.

Solara is located in Poway, an incorporated city 20 miles (32 km) inland from downtown San Diego. With a 2007 median sales price of $640,000 for a single-family home, the municipality faces an acute demand for affordable housing.

Green building has long been regarded as too costly for the affordable housing sector, despite the clear money-saving benefits for low-income households. At Solara, the developer applied practical and cost-effective green features—often off-the-shelf technologies—to construct high-performance buildings and a low-maintenance, sustainable site. The most striking feature, however, is the solar array that powers the project.

The 142-kilowatt system is designed to provide all the electricity required to power the development. Even during the summer periods of peak demand, Solara exports energy to the grid. The efficiency of the system allows the developer to offer utilities at no cost to the tenants, which protects low-income residents from volatility in energy prices. The solar panels are carefully concealed atop the carports and apartment roofs, hidden from view below—an aesthetic condition required by the city.

In keeping with sustainable development practices, the site design is very compact. Designed by Rodriguez Associates Architects & Planners, Solara consists of six two-story apartment buildings arranged along the perimeter of the property. In the middle of the site lies the community center, where landscaped pathways radiate outward, connecting structures and open space. Along the back of the property, a pedestrian pathway 400 feet (122 m) long offers vistas of the natural greenbelt and provides access to the adjacent park, playground, and riparian amenities. To offset the high density, the architect incorporated semiprivate courtyards, communal open space, and seating areas throughout the property.

DEVELOPMENT TEAM

Owner/Developer
Community HousingWorks
San Diego, California
www.chworks.org

Design Architect
Rodriguez Associates Architects &
   Planners, Inc.
San Diego, California
www.ra-architects.net

Landscape Architect
Ivy Landscape Architects, Inc.
San Diego, California
www.ivyla.com

JURY STATEMENT

Solara is California's first affordable housing project designed to be fully independent of the power grid. Its photovoltaic panels provide the electrical needs—free of charge—for 56 affordable rental units and a small community center. Located on a ground-leased infill site adjacent to a floodway, the project navigated a myriad of entitlement, community, and technical challenges, becoming a fully leased community of households committed to a green program.

The use of solar energy opened up nontraditional funding opportunities to the development team and maximized the returns on traditional tax credits: the use of renewable energy fetched an extra $400,000 in low-income housing tax credits; the state of California offered $409,000 in renewable energy rebates; and federal investment tax credits covered approximately 20 percent of the hard cost of the photovoltaic system. Ultimately, the $1.1 million cost of the photovoltaic panels was almost entirely covered by state and federal incentives rarely used in financing affordable housing.

The 56 rental units at Solara range from 659 to 1,023 square feet (61.2 to 95 m²), and each one-, two-, or three-bedroom unit is either accessible to disabled residents or adaptable to be. Every dwelling contains low–volatile organic compound carpeting, formaldehyde-free insulation, energy-efficient appliances, and dual-flush toilets. To regulate indoor temperatures, each building at Solara incorporates passive design elements, such as proper siting for solar radiation and cross ventilation, double-paned windows, solar shades, and a radiant barrier.

On site, there is no turf to be mowed, and the landscaping strikes a sustainable balance between drought-resistant Mediterranean ornamentals and species native to southern California. The varied roof angles allow rainwater to drain to multiple bioswales, rather than a single stormwater structure. Freon-less air-conditioning units cool the site during summer months, and in winter, the structures are centrally heated from a gas-fired tankless boiler.

When tenants enter into a lease at Solara, they must sign a Green Addendum and attend a mandatory green orientation. CHW has developed a 360° Green Curriculum, which is designed to promote environmental awareness and educate residents—including children. Public art installations—all made of recycled materials—serve to reinforce principles of sustainability and environmental stew-

ardship for the tenants. The green curriculum has become so successful that the developer is planning to unveil the program across its affordable housing portfolio.

The project faced a number of challenges: nearby residents voiced reservations commonly associated with affordable housing, such as the adverse effect on property values, the increase in crime, and the potential for unsightly design; the city required the development team to begin construction within a year of submitting initial site plans—an ambitious timetable for the entitlement of any development; and a number of variances for parking reduction and density increases had to be obtained in this time frame.

The confluence of renewable energy and sustainable design has resulted in a 95 percent reduction in greenhouse gas emissions compared with a similar multifamily complex, and Solara's energy efficiency exceeds California's stringent Title 24 Energy Efficiency Building Standards by 15 percent. Its practical and cost-effective design provides a model for green affordable housing nationwide, where budgets are traditionally tight.

PROJECT DATA

Website
www.chworks.org

Site Area
2.5 ac (1.0 ha)

Facilities
56 single-family units
90 surface parking spaces

Land Uses
residential, open space, parking

Start/Completion Dates
November 2005–April 2007

SITE PLAN

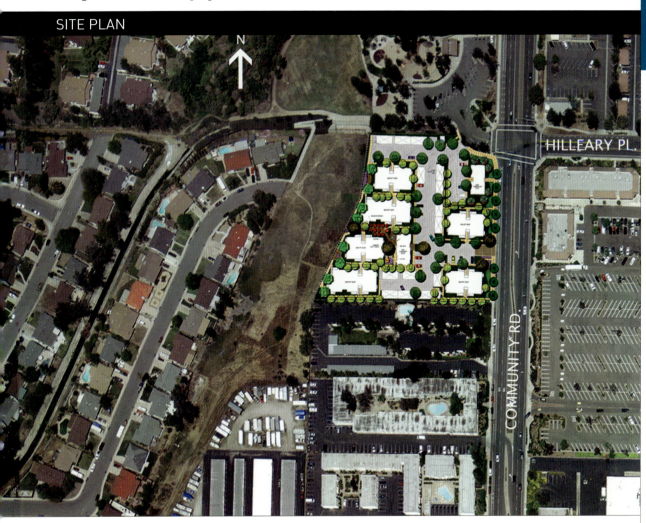

N

HILLEARY PL.

COMMUNITY RD.

Val d'Europe Downtown District

MARNE LA VALLÉE, FRANCE

Just as Walt Disney World in Orlando, Florida, has its new town of Celebration, Disneyland Park (née Euro Disney) has Val d'Europe. Both planned communities—Celebration and Val d'Europe—were established and designed on new urbanist principles, and both have transformed their respective regions. In 2008, eight years after Val d'Europe opened, the new community is 60 percent completed and scheduled to be built out by 2018. It is home to 21,000 residents.

Walt Disney, a pioneer in film animation, was a visionary entrepreneur who expanded the reach of his entertainment business to include a resort destination based on his animated films. With

JURY STATEMENT

As part of the development agreement between the state and the developer of Disneyland Park, 32 kilometers (20 mi) east of Paris, 1,943 hectares (4,801 ac) were set aside for a new town to support the resort destination. The Val d'Europe Downtown District, drawing on traditional French village design, attracts more than 20 million visitors annually.

DEVELOPMENT TEAM

Owner/Developer
Euro Disney Associés SCA
Marne la Vallée, France
www.eurodisney.com

Public Partners
SAN du Val d'Europe
Marne la Vallée, France
www.valeurope-sans.fr

EPA France
Marne la Vallée, France
www.marne-la-vallee.com

Developers
Value Retail PLC (La Vallée Village)
London, U.K.
www.valueretail.com

Ségécé (BNP-Paribus Group)
  (shopping mall)
Paris, France
www.segece.fr

Nexity SA (Place de Toscane)
Paris, France
www.nexity.fr

Master Planner
Cooper, Robertson & Partners
New York, New York
www.cooperrobertson.com

continued

Disneyland, his first theme park, his financial resources limited him to purchasing only enough land for the park itself; not he, but other developers capitalized on the ancillary developments that went up around Disneyland. With his second theme park, Walt Disney World, over 100 times Disneyland's area was secured at the start to ensure that Disney could capture the entirety of the resort destination's development potential. His successor company later applied this lesson at Disneyland Park.

The new town Val d'Europe began when the Walt Disney Company, flush with success at its first overseas version in Japan, chose a 1,943-hectare (4,801-ac) area in rural Marne la Vallée, 32 kilometers (20 mi) east of Paris, after a yearlong process of reviewing potential sites throughout Europe. Marne la Vallée was chosen in 1987 for its proximity to Paris, its central location in Europe at a junction of six major highways, the expectation of express rail lines into Paris, and a high-speed train (TGV) terminal, as well as the French government's willingness to partner with the developer. Euro Disney opened, amid controversy and hoopla, in April 1992. It was not immediately successful; planned for a daily visit count of 55,000 visitors, Euro Disney drew an average half that. But in 1995, tourism at the resort experienced a turnaround with the introduction of a new thrill ride, and as cultural opposition died down, the park started to show a profit, which has been sustained since.

To complement the Disney theme park concept in Europe, from the start Disney planned an adjacent new community, in part as a housing option for the 12,000 permanent employees that Disney

N

CHESSY

Quartier Nord /
North District

Quartier de la Gare /
Downtown District

TGV

COUPVRAY

Quartier des Lacs /
Lakeside District

LA

Quartier du Parc /
Parkside District

Parc Urbain /
Urban Park

Centre Commercial International /
International Mall

RER A

MONTEVRAIN

Zac des Gassets

Serris Village

SERRIS

BAILLY
ROMAINVILLIERS

AC

PHOTOGRAPHS BY YANNPIRIOU.COM (156); TIBO.ORG
(157, 158, 159TL, 159B, 161); CAROLE BARRIQUAND
(159TR); DISNEY (160).

projected for the park. In 1987, when Disney formed its operating unit to develop Euro Disney, the French government created a special state development company, called an Établissement Public d'Aménagement, to represent the public interest. The two parties negotiated a convention in which 150 hectares (371 ac) were set aside for a town center. A guiding principle was to create a framework of boulevards, streets, and large and small squares and parks to re-create the atmosphere of a traditional French town and to encourage density and walkability that would reduce the footprint of the town's built environment. The new town, serving the resort destination's tourists and employees, had to achieve a critical mass on an accelerated schedule to create a lively environment attractive to tourists, residents, and businesses.

Val d'Europe's town center is in three parts: Place de Toscane and Place d'Ariane (plazas for shops and restaurants, primarily to serve residents); Val d'Europe regional shopping center; and La Vallée Village (open-air, upmarket outlet shopping village). The TGV tracks bisect the town center, but a pedestrian main street one kilometer (0.62 mi) long crosses over them to connect Place de Toscane and Place d'Ariane on opposite sides of the tracks. The regional shopping center serves a rapidly growing region east of Paris, and the tourist-oriented La Vallée Village, selling luxury goods in an outlet format, is an innovation in France. La Vallée Village's developer, Value Retail, had pioneered upmarket outlet shopping elsewhere in Europe, and these high-end brands followed Value Retail to Val d'Europe, especially after the developer acquired special authorization from the French government to sell on Sundays in a country that generally does not permit that.

From the state's point of view, the economic return on its €550 million (US$817 million) investment (on infrastructure and other public improvements) has come in the form of €1 billion (US$1.47 billion) in direct tax proceeds from Euro Disney and €2.6 billion (US$3.8 billion) more from indirect sources (including VAT) within Disneyland Resort Paris and Val d'Europe since 1992. Other benefits include creating jobs (21,000 new jobs since 1992, directly attributable to Euro Disney, making it the largest employer in Seine-et-Marne); becoming Europe's top tourist destination with 14 million visitors annually; and encouraging a population rebalance in the Ile de France, as inhabitants have found new residential and employment options east of Paris.

PROJECT DATA

Websites
www.valdeurope.fr
www.valdeurope.com
www.lavalleevillage.com

Site Area
150 ha (371 ac)

Facilities
50,000 m² (538,196 sf) office space
  (300,000 m²/3,229,173 sf at
  buildout)
120,000 m² (1,291,669 sf) retail
  and restaurant space (150,000
  m2/1,614,586 sf at buildout)
1,847 residential units (6,000 at
  buildout)
6,500 parking spaces (shopping mall)

Land Uses
office, retail, restaurant,
  entertainment, hotel, residential,
  civic, education, parking, open
  space, conservation zones

Start/Completion Dates
1997–2000 (Phase I)

Carneros Inn

NAPA, CALIFORNIA

Located in the heart of Napa Valley's Carneros wine-growing region and surrounded on three sides by active vineyards, Carneros Inn is a 27-acre (11-ha) resort featuring 85 individual guest cottages, 24 vacation homes, restaurants, and ample meeting and event space. The second phase includes Carneros Town Square, which will consist of a post office and a food and wine market that will open the inn to the surrounding area. The first resort constructed in Napa County in over 20 years, Carneros Inn is the product of a decade-long planning initiative with the local government and residents of the agricultural community.

Carneros Inn is situated between the Sonoma and Napa wine regions of northern California, approximately 45 miles (72 km) northeast of San Francisco. Carneros Partners, founded by Keith Rogal, began its ten-year commitment in 1997, when the partnership began purchasing entitlements to the dilapidated mobile-home park that once stood in the midst of vineyards. The mobile homes were both an eyesore (in this tourism-heavy region) and an environmental liability; however, at the same time, they provided needed workforce housing, albeit of substandard quality.

Rather than seek a costly and complicated rezoning process, Carneros Partners pursued the novel concept of developing the luxury resort under existing regulations meant for low-density residential

DEVELOPMENT TEAM

Owners/Developers
Carneros Partners
San Francisco, California

Carneros Holding, LLC
Napa, California

Design Architect
William Rawn Associates,
  Architects, Inc.
Boston, Massachusetts
www.rawnarch.com

Landscape Architect
Olin Partnership
Philadelphia, Pennsylvania
www.olinptr.com

PROJECT DATA

Website
www.thecarnerosinn.com

Site Area
27 ac (10.9 ha)

Facilities
116,835 sf (10,854 m²) retail
24 single-family units
85 hotel rooms

Land Uses
hotel, residential, retail,
 restaurant, civic

Start/Completion Dates
2002–2007

use. The zoning laws in Napa County did not allow new construction to exceed the footprints of the original mobile homes or building foundations to be dug; to overcome these restrictions, the developer trucked in prefabricated, modular guest homes of identical square footage to replace the trailers.

Napa County residents and officials have long been wary of any new development in the region. At Carneros, the development team worked for years with the local community on issues of traffic impact and water usage that ultimately informed the design and programming of the property. For example, residents of Napa County—where freshwater is scarce—lobbied heavily for water conservation efforts. As a result, Carneros Inn includes a variety of water-saving features: an innovative tertiary treatment facility treats wastewater on site; the recycled graywater is then used to irrigate the approximately eight acres (3.2 ha) of landscaping, and drip-irrigation methods—more efficient than traditional spray-irrigation methods—are used on site. Carneros Inn also stores recycled water in two retention ponds, with provisions to release the surplus to a neighboring vineyard when necessary.

Designed by Boston-based William Rawn Associates, the resort is arranged around "Ward's Walk," a linear orchard that connects Carneros Town Square on the western end to the adjacent vineyard at the eastern end. The pathway offers an ever-present vista of the Napa section of the California Coast Range, reinforcing the region's deep agrarian roots. The civic square—which is under construction—will engage both local residents and guests of the resort, offering a post office, a market, a public restaurant, and additional meeting and conference space for the inn.

The simple board-and-batten guest cottages are capped with corrugated metal-clad roofing, consistent with the unadorned style of the traditional farming camps characteristic of the region. Each

cottage includes a private garden fenced off by corrugated metal and a front porch facing a common area, designed to foster interaction among guests. Groups of six to 12 guest cottages are organized around a landscaping feature, forming a single cluster. These central landscaped areas, designed by the Olin Partnership, are varied throughout the site, creating distinct identities for each collection of guest quarters.

At the highest point on the site, an iconic tower, reminiscent of a rural water tower, anchors one end of a porte cochere where guests check into the resort. Inside, a barnlike structure acts as the inn's dining room, accented by a barrel-vaulted roof monitor extending 40 feet (12 m) in length—another reference to an architectural feature native to the region's farm buildings—where clerestory windows admit light to the expansive space.

Carneros Inn, designed to strike a balance between the sophistication of modern-day Napa Valley and its rustic, agricultural roots, has been a financial and critical success. Despite its accolades, the luxury resort treads lightly amid its development-wary neighbors; barely visible from the roadway, the property is ringed by hedges, blending naturally with the rolling terrain.

PHOTOGRAPHS BY MARK HUNDLEY (162, 163L, 164); ART GRAY (163R, 165L, 165R)

Chimney Pot Park

SALFORD, UNITED KINGDOM

Located in Salford, an outer suburb of Manchester, Chimney Pot Park is a radical redevelopment of 349 residential units in a troubled terrace-house neighborhood. For years, the community suffered from low demand and declining value, and was plagued by crime and antisocial behavior, absentee landlords and irresponsible tenants, and open back alleys that encouraged neglect and vandalism. With the original housing stock slated for demolition, Urban Splash—a development company renowned for regenerating distressed or problematic sites—drastically reconfigured the internal design and layout of the homes while retaining the original façades and street pattern.

In 2001, the Seedley and Langworthy Partnership—composed of the Salford City Council, community stakeholders, and representatives from the police, public health organizations, the local housing association, and the schools—and Urban Splash developed a master plan to govern the redevelopment of the failed neighborhood and surrounding area. Recognizing that regenerating the neighborhood would entail acquiring the site in full, the local government used the innovative Homeswap

DEVELOPMENT TEAM

Owner/Developer
Urban Splash Limited
Manchester, United Kingdom
www.urbansplash.co.uk

Design Architect
shedkm ltd
Liverpool, United Kingdom
www.shedkm.co.uk

program. Under the scheme—the first of its kind in the United Kingdom—the Salford council allows homeowners to trade their distressed properties for a refurbished home nearby, transferring the mortgage to the new property. The local council used compulsory purchase orders—the United Kingdom's version of eminent domain—to acquire the remainder of the site.

Built in 1910, the homes at Chimney Pot Park are arranged in a traditional terraced grid on a dense, 3.2-hectare (7.9-ac) site, adjoining a community park to the south. Led by the architecture firm shedkm ltd, the design team retained the street patterns and brick façades, leaving the neighborhood with a familiar density, scale, and urban typology. The original brickwork was refurbished, and new double-glazed wood windows and doors were installed. The chimney stacks were reimagined as chimney roof lights, which permit ample daylighting and supply a modern aesthetic to the Victorian-era homes. The interior configuration and orientation to the street of each end unit was rotated 90 degrees to establish a new streetfront along the major access road.

The troublesome, open alleys were closed off and are now only accessible by secure, gated entrances at the ends of the terraces. At the rear of the units, garden decks extend over the covered parking at ground level, accommodating 50 percent of the site's parking requirements, with the remainder provided on the street. The new balconies create private areas for each unit, screened by landscaping and a linear herb garden.

Inside the two-story homes, the interior functions have been inverted: the ground floor now consists of two bedrooms and a bathroom rather than the living area seen in the traditional layout. The former attic space has been eliminated, replaced by a snug mezzanine level overlooking the upper-level living area. These upper levels feature interchangeable floor plans, with two layout choices for the kitchen, living room, and dining room. The expansive living area is now on the same level as the raised deck, allowing homeowners to extend their living space to encompass the private garden.

To overcome the perception that Urban Splash was engaging in "house-flipping"—that low-income housing was being purchased cheaply, renovated, and resold at a profit—the developer involved local community groups in the planning process from the beginning. All parties understood that wholesale changes were needed to stem the disinvestment seen in the Salford neighborhood. The original development agreement had reserved 50 units for low-income households; however, Urban Splash chose

Website
www.chimneypotpark.co.uk

Site Area
3.2 ha (7.9 ac)

Facilities
112 single-family units; 349 at
 buildout
113 parking spaces; 372 at buildout

Land Uses
residential, parking

Start/Completion Dates
October 2005–March 2007 (Phase I)

to market Chimney Pot Park through the country's First Time Buyers' Initiative—designed to enable those who cannot otherwise afford a new home—and 91 units were sold on an affordable basis.

Led by Urban Splash, the marketing campaign generated significant interest in the retrofitted development: in the first 2.5 hours of the launch in April 2006, 108 homes were sold. House prices started at £99,950 (US$195,000), and the highest price was £144,000 (US$281,500), well above the average house value of £20,000 to £30,000 (US$39,000 to US$58,700) in the area five years prior. Chimney Pot Park demonstrates that innovative design can change market perception of an area and provides an adaptable model for reusing existing housing stock to address community problems.

PHOTOGRAPHS BY PHOTOFLEX (166, 167L, 168); JOEL CHESTER FILDES (167R); URBAN SPLASH (169L); JONATHAN KEENAN (169TR); SHEDKM (169BR)

The Fifth Garden

SHENZHEN, CHINA

Located in the rapidly growing southern Chinese city of Shenzhen, bordering Hong Kong, the Fifth Garden represents a radical departure from the norm of recent urban residential development in China. Rather than fitting as many units as possible in a Western-style high-rise building or townhouse complex, Vanke Real Estate Company—mainland China's largest real estate developer—opted to celebrate Chinese tradition and design in its Fifth Garden project, a 11.2-hectare (27.7-ac) planned community containing 1,000 high-end for-sale residential units, a small commercial core, generous amounts of public open space, and parking for 750 cars.

Shenzhen, buoyed by its proximity to Hong Kong and attraction of foreign investment, has seen its population explode from 25,000 inhabitants to over 10 million residents in three decades. The Fifth Garden is located within a developing valley district, with green hills and a verdant landscape, lending the project a subtropical backdrop. The development is within 15 minutes of Shenzhen's booming downtown and has convenient transportation links to the rest of the city. Its closeness to downtown and attractive location make the Fifth Garden appealing for the growing number of affluent young professionals and families who live in Shenzhen.

DEVELOPMENT TEAM

Owner/Developer
Vanke Real Estate Company
Shenzhen, China
www.vanke.com

Master Planner/Landscape Architect
EDAW
San Francisco, California
www.edaw.com

Architect
Peddle Thorp Architects
Melbourne, Australia
www.pta.com.au

Local Architects
Beijing Institute of Architectural
  Design
Beijing, China
www.biad.com.cn

Bo'an Architectural Design
  Consultancy Company
Beijing, China

The Fifth Garden departs from the usual Western-influenced residential development seen in urban China, which lacks any relevance to culture and is often an incoherent amalgam of architectural styles and periods. Instead, the project team pursued a contemporary interpretation of the Chinese vernacular that embraces time-honored cultural sensibilities of scale, form, and importance of place. The goal of Vanke and its design team—master planner/landscape architect EDAW and architects Peddle Thorp Architects, the Beijing Institute of Architectural Design, and Bo'an Architectural Design Consultancy Company—was not to re-create a traditional village but to incorporate and express traditional elements within a modern context.

Their design integrates three components: a village center, townhouses and mid-rise apartments, and high-rise residential towers. The village center contains small shops, restaurants, and cafés, plus a relocated 300-year-old historic wood-frame house that serves as a teahouse and community center. All the residential structures are built around a series of gardens and courtyards that incorporate lush plantings, water features, walkways, and pavilions. Modeled on the classical designs of traditional Chinese gardens, the public spaces create opportunities for social interaction—places where children can play, adults can rendezvous, and neighbors can meet. The development's intriguing name refers to the four fabled gardens of Suzhou—here, in Shenzhen, one can live in the fifth garden.

In an effort to communicate the fusion between the traditional and the contemporary, the Fifth Garden's designers chose materials for the project carefully. White-washed walls, traditional gray brick, plants synonymous with Chinese culture (including bamboo and ficus trees), river pebbles, and natural stones convey the textures of a Chinese village. The use of glass and stainless steel creates a more modern atmosphere.

"Even as the Fifth Garden looks to history, it shows a new direction for residential landscape architecture in the region," says Sean Chiao, managing principal of EDAW in Asia. "It is a tasteful update of vernacular traditions. The design of the landscape is a departure from a lot of what we see in developing countries, where new residential development likes to imitate European or Western motifs and styles. At the Fifth Garden, we see a series of spaces searching for a unique identity that belongs to place, culture, and locale. For the Chinese market, it's exciting."

The Fifth Garden's traditional yet modern identity has been a hit with Shenzhen homebuyers. Its residences sold out soon after the project opened in July 2005, and property values rose more than 50 percent in the project's first 18 months. The developer's return on cost is estimated to be 50 percent. Other projects now underway elsewhere in China are attempting to achieve the Fifth Garden's combination of a unique design, ample public space, and strong property values. As a result, a dose of serenity and indigenous aesthetics is being injected into the nation's increasingly frenetic cities.

PROJECT DATA

Website
http://village.vanke.com

Site Area
11.2 ha (27.7 ac)

Facilities
3,500 m² (37,674 sf) retail
1,000 single-family units
750 parking spaces

Land Uses
residential, retail, restaurants,
 parks/open space

Start/Completion Dates
February 2003–July 2005

New Columbia

PORTLAND, OREGON

In 2003, Columbia Villa was an aging, distressed 462-unit public housing development in Portland, Oregon. The pre–World War II public housing project suffered from substandard construction—the homes were built to last only ten years—as well as inadequate infrastructure and inaccessibility for the physically disabled.

Today, the neighborhood—rebranded as New Columbia—is nearly twice as dense with 854 mixed-income units on site, including 232 new homeownership units, 186 affordable rental units, and 370 public housing and Section 8 rental units. The residential component is so well mixed, in fact, that differentiating between market-rate and subsidized housing is difficult. The commercial "Main Street" offers shops, an elementary school, a Boys & Girls Clubs of America, community college classrooms, and two mixed-use structures expected to achieve a LEED (Leadership in Energy and Environmental Design) Silver certification.

The financing for New Columbia was an intricate constellation of grants, loans, tax credits, and tax-exempt bonds. Seeded by a $35 million U.S. Department of Housing and Urban Development (HUD) HOPE VI grant in 2002, the Housing Authority of Portland (HAP) redevelopment effort almost immediately encountered roadblocks: first, the HUD Demolition Grant program was unexpectedly withdrawn

DEVELOPMENT TEAM

Owner/Developer
Housing Authority of Portland
Portland, Oregon
www.hapdx.org

Master Planner
Mithun
Seattle, Washington
www.mithun.com

Design Architect
Michael Willis Architects
Portland, Oregon
www.mwaarchitects.com

SITE PLAN

NEW STREET GRID

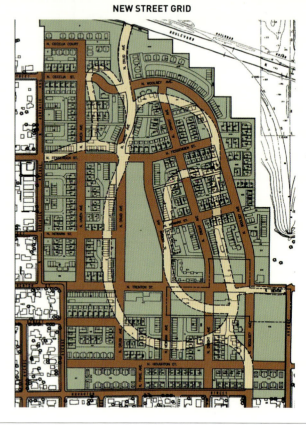

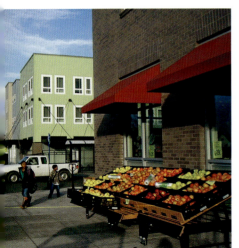

PHOTOGRAPHS BY PETE ECKERT (174); JULIE KEEFE (175L); MIKE WERT, HOUSING AUTHORITY OF PORTLAND (175R, 177); PAMELA KAMBUR, HOUSING AUTHORITY OF PORTLAND (176L); MITHUN (176LC); HOUSING AUTHORITY OF PORTLAND (176R)

nationwide, leaving a $5 million funding gap; and, second, a new school was desperately needed in the New Columbia neighborhood—an expense not considered in the original budget.

To overcome the shortfall, HAP used a blended-finance approach, melding new programs with established financing tools, including low-income housing tax credit allocations, tax-exempt bond financing, and conventional construction loans. HAP also enlisted the aid of private foundations, grants, and loan programs, such as the Federal Home Loan Bank, the Bill & Melinda Gates Foundation, the Paul G. Allen Family Foundation, and Meyer Memorial Trust. In response to the need for a new school, HAP pioneered the first use of New Market Tax Credits for an elementary school, completing construction in 11 months—just in time for the first day of school in September 2006.

Originally built in 1942, the curving, suburban street pattern of the original design cordoned off Columbia Villa from greater Portland, leaving the development physically isolated from surrounding neighborhoods. The New Columbia master plan, executed by the urban planning and architecture firm Mithun, designed the new street network to reconnect to the existing grid—with 12 street connections rather than the previous four—knitting the new mixed-income community back into the urban fabric.

HAP was determined to completely reinvent the New Columbia neighborhood: it oversaw the demolition of over 400,000 square feet (37,161 m²) of inadequate housing, the removal and replacement of the subterranean infrastructure system, and a complete reconfiguration of the street system. More than 1,300 residents had to be moved before their new homes could be built, lending urgency to the completion of the project.

The original Columbia Villa site was home to 430 mature trees, many planted during the original construction. More than 50 percent of the existing trees were preserved during construction—a remarkable feat, considering that the location of many trees conflicted with the new street-grid system. Capitalizing on the natural 2 percent north-to-south slope on the 82-acre (33-ha) site, all stormwater is collected, treated, and infiltrated on site rather than flushed into the overtaxed public sewer system or the environmentally fragile Columbia Slough. This "green street" system includes approximately 100 bioswales, 32 filter boxes, and drywells strategically placed at every intersection. A four-acre (1.62-ha) city park, four pocket parks, common greens, and public gardens complete the greenery that proliferates on site.

HAP ensured that the demolition and reconstruction of New Columbia became an economic engine for the community: over $100 million in contracts was apportioned to local firms; over 20 percent of all construction work was awarded to disadvantaged, minority-owned, women-owned, and emerging small businesses; and the project created 104 construction-related jobs for low-income residents from the neighborhood. Now that 82 acres (33 ha) of obsolete, underused public housing—once a constant drain on public resources—has been transformed into a balanced, functional community, HAP can turn its attention to other housing needs throughout the Portland region.

New Columbia was conceived, designed, and built by a remarkable coalition of residents, neighbors, homebuilders, public and nonprofit agencies, and private sector financial partners. Frequently, such a diverse group of stakeholders is perceived as antithetical to the swift and economic management of a project; however, the New Columbia project was completed within its budget and two months ahead of schedule.

PROJECT DATA

Website
www.newcolumbia.org

Site Area
82 ac (32 ha)

Facilities
17,507 sf (1,627 m²) office
3,937 sf (366 m²) retail
232 single-family units
622 multifamily units
832 surface parking spaces

Land Uses
office, residential, retail, restaurant, civic, education, parks/open space, parking

Start/Completion Dates
2002–October 2006

Savannah CondoPark

SINGAPORE

Flanked by columns ten meters (33 ft) tall on which hieroglyphic animals are carved, and set in lush landscaping with a menagerie of bronze animal sculptures, the gateway that welcomes residents and visitors to Savannah CondoPark dramatically sets the stage for this sustainable, safari adventure–themed community. Inside the gates, 18 ten-story condominium buildings, with footprints totaling 23 percent of the 5.5-hectare (13.6-ac) site, curve around a four-hectare (ten-ac) common open space featuring pools, gardens, and terraces.

Completed in September 2005, the 99-year-leasehold residential community contains 648 two- to five-bedroom condominium apartments. Because of height restrictions imposed by the nearby airport, the units are housed in 18 ten-story buildings, which are arranged in two arcing blocks opposite each other, enclosing the central open space. The development incorporates a wide range of amenities, including nature trails, trellised walkways, children's play areas, tennis courts, fitness

DEVELOPMENT TEAM

Owner/Developer
City Developments Limited
Singapore
www.cdl.com.sg

Architect
AXIS Architects Planners
Singapore
http://axisarch.com.sg

Landscape Architect
Cicada Pte Ltd
Singapore
www.cicada.com.sg

stations, pools, waterfalls, barbecue facilities, and—in its clubhouse—a bowling alley, game room, and gymnasium.

The safari theme not only provides a backstory for the project but also creates a green development platform that unifies the community's residential buildings. City Developments Limited (CDL)'s focus on environmental sustainability led to the use of sustainable or recycled products wherever possible—an uncommon practice in Singapore. The partition walls were made of recycled gypsum, doors and wardrobes are composed of recycled materials, and the bronze animal sculptures were precast using recycled copper cables.

The site, which is landlocked by an expressway and high-rise condominium buildings, offers no outward views. AXIS Architects Planners designed a natural earthen wall, rather than the unsightly concrete acoustic barriers traditionally used to block the busy highway, and oriented Savannah CondoPark's buildings to face a central area, known as the community zone, that contains most of the project's recreational features and open space. The site design responds to the area's tropical climate by providing extensive shade within the community zone and offering optimal natural lighting in the residences.

The housing units feature energy-saving air-conditioning systems and planter boxes with built-in water taps that allow residents to enjoy outdoor gardening even on upper floors. Photovoltaic panels on the roof of the clubhouse generate supplemental electricity, which is used for clubhouse lighting, heating, and air conditioning. A pneumatic waste-disposal system transfers solid waste from the resi-

dential units to central sealed compactors, while conveniently placed recycling bins encourage residents to recycle, and plentiful bicycle racks encourage the use of bikes. Residents receive a guide that explains the green features found in their units and throughout the community, as well as a book that promotes green living.

Calling the development Singapore's first eco-condo, Eddie Wong, general manager in the projects division of CDL, says that Savannah CondoPark "is an environmental, social, and commercial success. It was designed to answer the government's call to provide affordable, entry-level private housing in Singapore, where about 80 percent of the population lives in subsidized government housing—but also to give its residents a standard of quality and amenities on a par with luxury projects. Savannah CondoPark was crafted with environmental sustainability in mind, from the development stage through the entire lifespan of the building. The result is a project of exceptional quality and value-added features that are eco-friendly as well as a hit with buyers. The positive eco-impact and the ripples of green influence we hope we have achieved for the environment through this project are immeasurable."

At Savannah CondoPark, CDL has proven that green development can be profitable as well as socially responsible. By emphasizing high standards of construction—which were achieved partly through prefabrication—the developer saved time and money, enhanced the project's quality, and created a healthier environment for workers and residents. The unit construction cost of SG$883 per square meter (US$53 per sf) was significantly lower than the local industry average for standard mid-rise condominiums.

Savannah CondoPark has been presented Singapore's Green Mark Award for sustainable design and has received the highest-ever CONQUAS score—the national benchmark for construction quality. CDL hopes the project will serve as a model for green residential development efforts locally and elsewhere; in fact, in December 2006, the Singaporean government announced a program of cash incentives to motivate developers to "go green."

PROJECT DATA

Website
http://savannah.cdl.com.sg

Site Area
5.5 ha (13.6 ac)

Facilities
648 multifamily units
749 parking spaces

Land Uses
residential, recreation, parks/open
space

Start/Completion Dates
February 2003–September 2005

CIVIC

PHOTOGRAPHS BY: JEFF GOLDBERG, ESTO PHOTOGRAPHICS (L); URBAN REDEVELOPMENT AUTHORITY SINGAPORE (LC); JEFF GOLDBERG, ESTO PHOTOGRAPHICS (LR); JOHN TROTTO, JOHN TROTTO PHOTOGRAPHY (R)

Bras Basah.Bugis

SINGAPORE

The district now known as Bras Basah.Bugis, located northeast of Singapore's city center, was once an area characterized by low real estate values and deteriorating physical conditions. In 1989, the Urban Redevelopment Authority (URA) of Singapore, the national planning authority, in partnership with private developers, embarked on a two-decade redevelopment effort to transform the area into the city-state's arts, culture, learning, and entertainment district. Today, the 95-hectare (235-ac) district is home to a synergistic educational and arts cluster—three national museums, seven arts housing facilities, three arts schools, 105 private commercial schools, a city university, and a new National Library—as well as a vibrant mixed-use core, including 266,700 square meters (2.87 million sf) of office space, 141,300 square meters (1.52 million sf) of retail space, and more than 1,100 residential units.

A commercial development, Bugis Junction, was the first project completed in accordance with URA's redevelopment plan. URA encouraged the developer to recapture the essence of the low-rise

DEVELOPMENT TEAM

Public Agency
Urban Redevelopment Authority
Singapore
www.ura.gov.sg

JURY STATEMENT

Bras Basah.Bugis is a shining example of Singapore's redevelopment strategy to constantly update its urban design and infrastructure through a collaborative approach involving government organizations, private enterprises, and public representatives. The quarter-century-long program has transformed this distressed, deteriorating area—through a balance of free-market economics and public planning—into a vibrant mixed-use district of arts, culture, learning, and entertainment.

shop house form characteristic of Southeast Asia, as well as a series of "internal streets," to integrate the complex into the surrounding neighborhood. The resulting project—built in 1989 and retrofitted in 2004—features glass-covered shopping arcades with traditional ground-floor shops and restaurants on a 3.7-hectare (9.1-ac) city block. The 90-meter (295-ft) main spine of the barrel-vaulted, three-story arcade encloses Bugis Street and is adjacent to a mass rapid-transit station.

In a traditionally mixed area, with shops, schools, and places of worship, URA saw an enormous opportunity to capitalize on the district's rich architectural and cultural heritage. The national planning authority identified and safeguarded four significant places of worship as National Monuments within the district. Also, URA slated three 1850s-era schools—well known for their distinct architectural styles—for adaptive use. Two of the structures were reused to create a cluster of museums, while the third was transformed into a cloistered village with al fresco restaurants and bars, and boutiques and galleries.

The district redevelopment—named for two streets with commercial identities, Bras Basah and Bugis—features innovative projects that retain the local character of the district, creating a neighborhood that is well loved by locals and tourists alike. Two main streets in the district—Albert and Waterloo—were converted to pedestrian only, engendering a colorful and vibrant street life. Waterloo Street has been reimagined as Singapore's "arts belt"—a five-year, SG$7 million (US$5.1 million) public investment yielded affordable, unique housing for art students studying at nearby universities and gallery space to showcase the city-state's eclectic arts scene.

URA's vision for Bras Basah.Bugis depended on the partnership of private developers. The national planning authority meets regularly with private investors, gathering feedback to understand the needs of the market. Since 1970, the value of all of the government-owned land sold in the Bras Basah.Bugis district has increased to approximately SG$3 billion (US$2.2 billion). Also, URA has attracted strong bids from both local and foreign investors in the redevelopment area. In 2007, a consortium including local developer City Developments Limited, Dubai-based Isithmar Group, and the U.S. corporation El-Ad Group invested SG$1.69 billion (US$1.2 billion) to develop a mixed-use project on a 3.5-hectare (8.6-ac) parcel.

URA also conducted extensive consultation with community stakeholders during the master-plan development for the Bras Basah.Bugis district. URA architects held briefings for the local

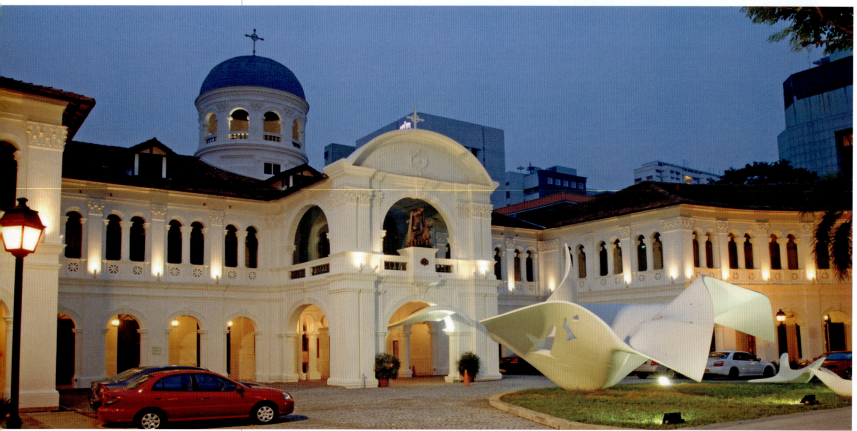

community, grassroots groups, and political leaders, and a public survey was used to obtain feedback on proposals. For example, because of concerns from religious leaders, an open space was retained in front of the temples' entrances on Waterloo Street to cater to the throngs that congregate during festivals.

The SG$600 million (US$440 million) investment by the city-state to transform the Bras Brasah. Bugis district into an educational and cultural hub has yielded impressive results: the area now has an academic population of more than 12,000 students and 1,500 teaching staff, the new National Library has experienced a 50 percent increase in readership, and the National Museum of Singapore's visitorship has tripled since its refurbishment. In economic terms, the regenerative plan has also been successful: the vacancy rate for office space has decreased from 10.4 percent in 2000 to 8.6 percent in 2007, median rents in the same sector have increased by 31 percent, and median rents for retail space have risen by 17 percent.

SITE PLAN

PROJECT DATA

Website
www.ura.gov.sg/cudd/cawebsite/
bugis-intro.htm

Site Area
95 ha (235 ac)

Facilities
50,181 m² (540,144 sf) education
38,000 m² (409,029 sf) arts-related
   space
30,000 m² (322,917 sf) museum
266,700 m² (2.87 million sf) office
141,300 m² (1.52 million sf) retail
1,192 multifamily units
3,129 hotel rooms
1,120 parking spaces

Land Uses
office, retail, residential, hotel,
   entertainment, civic, education,
   restaurant, parks/open space

Start/Completion Dates
1989–present

PHOTOGRAPHS BY AEDAS PTE LTD/ FOSTER
& PARTNERS (184); URBAN REDEVELOPMENT
AUTHORITY SINGAPORE (185, 186L; 186R, 187L, 188T,
188B, 189); NATIONAL LIBRARY BOARD (187R)

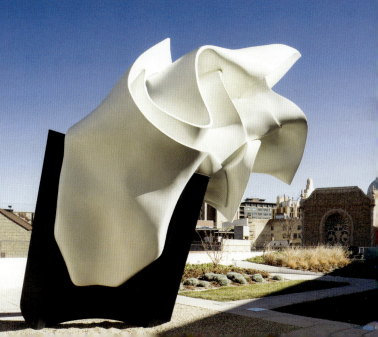

Overture Center for the Arts

MADISON, WISCONSIN

Completed in April 2006, the 400,000-square-foot (37,161-m²) Overture Center for the Arts project includes Overture Hall, a new world-class performance-arts facility; the Madison Museum of Contemporary Art, an expanded art museum; and a variety of renovated performance and visual arts spaces. Set on an urban infill site just one block from the Wisconsin state capitol building, the center was made possible by a gift of $210 million—one of the largest gifts for an arts center in the United States—from W. Jerome Frautschi, a retired local businessman.

DEVELOPMENT TEAM

Owner/Developer
Overture Development Corporation
Madison, Wisconsin
www.overturecenter.com

Architect
Pelli Clarke Pelli Architects
New Haven, Connecticut
www.pcparch.com

JURY STATEMENT

The Overture Center brings to one location—an entire city block just steps away from the state capitol building—seven performing arts companies, four visual arts organizations, and a new museum. The common operations and shared spaces create an economy of scale, saving the public from supporting far-flung organizations, and add to the critical mass of downtown activity. Underwritten primarily by one benefactor, the W. Jerome Frautschi family, the Overture Center's development and ownership structure is a replicable model for arts districts everywhere.

The Overture Center occupies the 2.5-acre (one-ha) site of the former Madison Civic Center in downtown Madison. The new civic facility fronts State Street, one of the four main axes originating from the State Capitol of Wisconsin. In addition to satisfying some of the community's unmet cultural needs, Overture Center for the Arts has accelerated the revitalization of central Madison.

By renovating and significantly expanding the city's former cultural arts center (the Madison Civic Center), the Overture Center project has created an exciting new destination comprising seven performance venues, four art galleries, and a museum of contemporary art. Developed and owned by the private nonprofit Overture Development Corporation, the arts center is operated by the Madison Cultural Arts District, a public sector entity.

George E. Austin, president of the Overture Development Corporation, calls Overture Center for the Arts "a once-in-a-lifetime project, combining the power of a civic vision with the generosity of a

PHOTOGRAPHS BY JEFF GOLDBERG, ESTO
PHOTOGRAPHICS

local citizen and a historic partnership among the city of Madison and its local arts organizations to plan, design, build, and operate this new Madison landmark. Together, the elaborate public/private partnership created a place of beauty and substance in which the community can celebrate its artistic spirit and dreams, anchoring a cultural-arts district in the heart of the city for the enjoyment of all for generations to come."

In a sense, planning for Overture Center for the Arts began when the Madison Civic Center—home to Madison Symphony Orchestra, Madison Opera, Madison Repertory Theatre, and Madison Arts Center—opened in 1980. By the late 1990s, this facility was no longer able to meet the needs of the arts community. Frautschi's gift, announced in 1998, was made in conjunction with the city's Downtown 2000 Plan, which called for expanding cultural facilities and activities to increase their role in the city's downtown revitalization strategy.

The architect for Overture Hall, Cesar Pelli of Pelli Clarke Pelli Architects, blended old and new in one structure and created a variety of spaces large and small, formal and informal. By preserving the façade of a former department store—the only designated historic structure on the block—the new building respects the design qualities of the city's shopping district and offers a pedestrian-friendly face while accommodating a 2,250-seat performance hall. Topped with a crystalline dome that allows natural light to penetrate all four interior levels, the multistory rotunda inside the entrance links Overture Hall with the expanded and renamed Madison Museum of Contemporary Art. In addition to its main performance space, Overture Hall—the lobby of which is enclosed by a curtain wall of insulating glass—includes three small, flexible "black box" theaters for rehearsals, intimate stage performances, readings, and other such events.

The Overture Center project was carried out in two phases, enabling arts organizations to continue to put on performances while construction was underway. Phase 2 included the renovation of the former civic center facilities and the expansion of the Madison Museum of Contemporary Art, which contains a new lecture hall, a rooftop sculpture garden, and a restaurant.

The project's financial plan was almost as complex as its design and programming. The city required that the completed facility be publicly operated, but it was not willing to incur significant additional taxpayer expense. Consequently, Frautschi's gift was leveraged to secure financing for the development of Overture Center as well as to provide operating funds for the completed project. The redevelopment authority transferred city-owned property, including the former civic center, for $1 to Overture Development Corporation, which then leased it back to the Madison Cultural Arts District, an agency created by the city to operate Overture Center for the Arts. When the construction bonds are retired in 2036, Overture Development Corporation will transfer the center to the Madison Cultural Arts District for $1.

PROJECT DATA

Website
www.overturecenter.com

Site Area
2.5 ac (1.0 ha)

Facilities
400,000 sf (37,161 m²) arts and
  related space

Land Uses
performing arts/museum/galleries,
  office, retail, restaurant, civic,
  education

Start/Completion Dates
June 2001–April 2006

Chaparral Water Treatment Facility

SCOTTSDALE, ARIZONA

Located in Scottsdale, Arizona, the 76,000-square-foot (7,061-m²) Chaparral Water Treatment Facility was built to meet the current and future water demand of this desert city and Phoenix suburb. Through the use of cutting-edge technology, the facility fulfills its public mandate on a minimal footprint and lessens its impact on the neighboring community with art and sculpture that pay homage to desert life. Completed in June 2006, the result transforms a necessary community resource—typically relegated to industrial areas—into a backdrop for the bustling Chaparral Park.

In the 1970s, the Scottsdale community approved a $10 million bond to fund the 30-year Indian Bend Wash project, a plan to upgrade the flood-prone, 12-mile (19-km) greenbelt that runs through Scottsdale. The area, referred to as the "slough," was routinely inundated during infrequent but nevertheless heavy rains, leaving the center of Scottsdale susceptible to flash floods. Today, the floodway provides an extensive recreational area for the community, while still serving its primary function—channeling floodwaters away from the city and toward the Salt River. Located on the northernmost end of the greenbelt, the Chaparral Water Treatment Facility stands as the capstone of the public works project, completing the 30-year vision of the Indian Bend Wash plan.

DEVELOPMENT TEAM

Owner/Developer
City of Scottsdale
Scottsdale, Arizona
www.scottsdaleaz.gov

Architect
Swaback Partners PLLC
Scottsdale, Arizona
www.swabackpartners.com

Landscape Architect
Ten Eyck Landscape Architects
Phoenix, Arizona
www.teneyckla.com

PROJECT DATA

Website
www.scottsdaleaz.gov

Site Area
29 ac (11.7 ha)

Facilities
3,000 sf (279 m²) office
73,000 sf (6782 m²) industrial

Land Uses
office, industrial, civic, education,
parks/open space

Start/Completion Dates
January 2004–June 2006

Situated on a nine-acre (3.6-ha) floodplain, the Chaparral Water Treatment Facility is located in a highly populated area of Scottsdale, making community acceptance of the building critical. Built to eliminate the municipality's dependence on water purchased from the city of Phoenix, the public facility uses state-of-the-art technologies to control noise and odor and operates with minimal staff. These advanced techniques allow a much smaller footprint—the plant is one-third to one-half the size of comparable water treatment facilities. Despite its size, the facility has a capacity of more than 30 million gallons per day, meeting future demand and complying with Scottsdale's 100-year assured water supply plan.

An overarching design concept was developed to soften the transition between Chaparral Park—directly adjacent to the water treatment facility—and the busy arterial to the plant's north, as well as to mitigate the effect of the facility's industrial elements on the nearby neighborhood. On the side facing the four-lane thoroughfare, the designers—led by Swaback Partners and Ten Eyck Landscape Architects—addressed the grade change from the building perimeter to the street through landscaped terraces defined by gabion walls, which are rectangular, wire-mesh cages containing indigenous rocks. Weathered, woven-metal structures are positioned at intervals along the frontage, an artistic nod to the site's industrial nature. The facility itself is clad in rough-hewn masonry, reflecting the rugged environment of the surrounding Sonoran Desert.

Designed to promote an appreciation of desert art and culture, the earthen-hued sculptures that proliferate at Chaparral Park seize upon a leitmotif of shade and shadow. More than 16,000 square feet (1,486 m²) of tensile canopies provide relief from the sun throughout the park, while architecturally representing nomadic desert dwellings of the past. Monumental-scale metal panels, which are combined with woven mesh, project shadow forms that change according to the sun's path and represent the water filtration process behind a wall that is 30 feet (9.1 m) high and 320 feet (98 m) long.

The Chaparral Water Treatment Facility transitions into an extensive recreation area, Chaparral Park, situated along 20 acres (8.1 ha) of the Indian Bend Wash. The popular park includes a Xeriscape Demonstration Garden, landscaped large open spaces, running trails, a dog park, and two multiuse ball fields. The xeriscape garden doubles as an educational tool for the public about water conservation principles and drought-resistant plants. Various water features and dramatic gardens are incorporated into the park as part of the Scottsdale Public Art Program.

The total construction cost for the Chaparral Water Treatment Facility was $65.5 million, including $8.2 million worth of improvements to the intersection adjacent to the plant and $6.2 million to upgrade Chaparral Park. The water treatment facility was funded through bond sales backed by water development fees and user rates, and the funds for the intersection and park improvements were supplied by separate municipal bonds.

PHOTOGRAPHS BY JOHN TROTTO, JOHN TROTTO
PHOTOGRAPHY (196, 197R, 198C, 198R, 199T, 199B);
BILL TIMMERMAN, TIMMERMAN PHOTOGRAPHY
(197L, 198L)

The Americas Jury

Marilee A. Utter, Jury Chair
Denver, Colorado

Marilee Utter is founder and president of Citiventure Associates LLC, a Denver-based real estate advisory firm specializing in public/private transactions and offering expertise in transit-oriented development and mixed-use villages. In addition to having experience as a banker (Wells Fargo Bank) and as a private developer (Trillium Corporation, managing the revitalization of Denver's Central Platte Valley railyards), she has worked on the establishment of the Office of Asset Management for the City and County of Denver and the establishment of the Department of Transit-Oriented Development for the (Denver) Regional Transit District.

With this wide-ranging background, Utter has become a nationally known speaker, writer, and adviser on innovative approaches and implementation strategies for complex urban projects.

Utter holds an MBA from UCLA's Anderson School, a certificate in state and local public policy from Harvard's Kennedy School, and the Counselor of Real Estate (CRE) designation. She is a Fellow in the Royal Institution of Chartered Surveyors, trustee of the Urban Land Institute, and chair of ULI's Colorado District Council.

Ronald A. Altoon
Los Angeles, California

Ronald Altoon is founding design partner of Altoon + Porter Architects, LLP, an international architectural, urban design, and planning firm with professional practice entities in Los Angeles, Amsterdam, Shanghai, Hong Kong, and Moscow. He is responsible for designs for complex projects in Asia, Australia, the Middle East, Europe, and the United States.

Altoon's practice encompasses urban infill, retail, commercial mixed-use, higher education, transit, and residential projects. He has authored three books on the work of his firm, as well as two for the retail industry on international projects and the influence of context and culture on design.

A ULI leader, Altoon served on the ULI New York World Trade Center Summit 2006 Blue Ribbon Panel and speaks at ULI conferences, both domestic and international. He was national president in 1998 of the American Institute of Architects. He holds a bachelor's degree in architecture from the University of Southern California and a master's degree in architecture from the University of Pennsylvania.

Thomas Cody
Portland, Oregon

Tom Cody is a principal at Gerding Edlen, a Portland-based development company. He is responsible for the firm's California business and is involved in new business development, project planning, financing, and expanding education-related developments and other government facilities and public/private partnerships. Cody has developed numerous student housing projects, a Health Professions Campus for Pacific University, The Civic (in Portland, Oregon), and South Park (co-developed in Los Angeles with Williams & Dame Development).

Cody has extensive experience in city planning, architecture, and development. He earned a master's degree in urban planning from Harvard University and a bachelor of science degree in urban planning and development from the University of Southern California. He also worked for Pritzker Prize–winning architect Frank O. Gehry and is currently the chairman of the board of trustees of Oregon Ballet Theater.

Timur Fisk Galen
New York, New York

Timur Galen is a managing director at Goldman Sachs & Company, where he functions as global head of corporate services and real estate.

Prior to joining Goldman Sachs in 2002, Galen worked as an executive with the Walt Disney Company and Reichmann International, LP. He is a registered architect, having completed his design apprenticeship with Pritzker Prize–winning architects Robert Venturi (Venturi, Scott Brown and Associates) and Fumihiko Maki.

Galen is a trustee of MASS MoCA and a director of the Forum for Urban Design and the Alliance for Downtown New York. He is a member of ULI and serves on the boards of the Steven Newman Real Estate Institute, Baruch College/The City University of New York, and the Property Committee of Inwood House. He is also past chair of the Haverford College Annual Fund and serves on the college's National Gifts Program Committee.

Galen earned master's degrees in architecture and civil and urban engineering from the University of Pennsylvania in 1984. He was a Henry Luce Foundation research fellow at Tokyo University in 1982 and 1983 and received his bachelor's degree in physics from Haverford College in 1978.

Richard M. Gollis
Newport Beach, California

Richard M. Gollis is cofounder and principal of The Concord Group, a strategic real estate advisory firm that works with the nation's leading developers and financial institutions to maximize the value of land use opportunities. The Concord Group covers the analysis of all asset classes, with an emphasis on market and financial strategies for complex, multiuse projects and large-scale land development. The firm maintains offices in Newport Beach, San Francisco, and Boston and is active throughout the United States, Central America, and the Caribbean.

Gollis is active in the Urban Land Institute in many capacities. He currently chairs the Community Development Council (Blue Flight) and is a member of the Policy and Practice Committee. He is a governor of the ULI Foundation and serves as a District Council Counselor. In his local community, Gollis cochairs the Advisory Board for the University of California at Irvine's Policy and Planning Department and serves on the boards of several nonprofit organizations in leadership capacities. A Boston native, Gollis is a graduate of Brown University with a degree in international relations.

Gary Hack
Philadelphia, Pennsylvania

Gary Hack is immediate past dean of the School of Design, University of Pennsylvania and continues at Penn as the Paley Professor of City and Regional Planning. He has practiced urban design in more than 40 world cities, focusing on waterfront planning, mixed-use developments, residential developments, and downtown revitalization. His projects include planning the redevelopment of Prudential Center Boston (a ULI Global Award winner), planning the West Side Waterfront in New York and Rockefeller Park at Battery Park City, and a new metropolitan plan for Bangkok, Thailand. Hack collaborated with Studio Libeskind on the winning design for rebuilding the World Trade Center in New York.

Hack has also taught at Penn and at MIT. His books include coauthorship of *Site Planning*, *Global City Regions*, and *Urban Design in an International Context*. He has served as chair of the Philadelphia City Planning Commission and serves on many boards.

Hack received his BArch from the University of Manitoba, an MArch and MUP from the University of Illinois, and a PhD in urban studies and planning from MIT. In 2006, he was awarded an honorary Doctor of Laws degree from Dalhousie University.

Veronica W. Hackett
New York, New York

Veronica Hackett is managing partner of the Clarett Group, a New York–based real estate company that develops mixed-use properties in urban areas. During her career, Hackett has developed over 13 million square feet (1.2 million m²) of real estate in New York and worldwide. Clarett Capital, formed with Prudential Real Estate Investors, currently has active development projects in New York, Los Angeles, and Washington, D.C., ranging in size from 150,000 to 1 million square feet (14,000 to 93,000 m²).

In addition to her work as a private sector developer, Hackett has been a corporate real estate executive in the United States and Europe, a real estate pension fund asset manager, a real estate lender, a Wall Street financial analyst, and a CIA economic analyst. She is a trustee of ULI and serves on the board of directors of the Real Estate Board of New York, the New York University Real Estate Institute, and the New York Building Congress. Hackett received her master's degree in finance from New York University and a bachelor's degree in history and economics from the College of Notre Dame of Maryland.

William H. Kreager
Seattle, Washington

In a career spanning 30-plus years, Bill Kreager has created new homes and communities across the United States. The focus of his practice, as principal at Mithun and as a LEED-accredited professional, is the integration of site planning, building design, and sustainability in urban infill and mixed-use developments. His projects have achieved national recognition for smart growth implementation, environmentally sensitive master site planning, and innovative architectural design. His progressive, market-oriented projects range from small, infill communities to new 6,000-acre (2,428-ha) towns.

Kreager has been lead master planner for innovative new communities throughout the Pacific Northwest, and he speaks on housing issues before regional and national audiences.

J. Michael Pitchford
Washington, D.C.

J. Michael Pitchford presently serves as the president and CEO of Community Preservation and Development Corporation (CPDC). Founded in 1989, CPDC is a 501(c)(3) organization dedicated to expanding the supply of affordable housing in the mid-Atlantic region. It has completed more than 3,500 units of housing and has more than 1,300 units currently in its pipeline.

Previously, Pitchford led the Community Development Equity Group at Bank of America Corporation in Charlotte, North Carolina, which, during his ten-year tenure, developed or rehabilitated 23,000 units of affordable housing and increased equity commitments 3,000 percent.

He also has led or participated in workshops, conferences, and forums on housing policy, community development, and the sharing of best practices. He serves on the boards of the National Equity Fund, the National Housing Conference, and the Center for Housing Policy. Pitchford is the immediate past chairman of the Affordable Housing Council of ULI and was a past chairman of the National Housing Conference. He earned his bachelor's and master's degrees from Old Dominion University.

Christopher Glenn Sawyer
Atlanta, Georgia

Christopher Glenn Sawyer is a partner with the law firm of Alston & Bird LLP in Atlanta, Georgia, where he advises clients on issues relating to corporate governance, strategic planning, the environment, and real estate. He currently serves as an emeritus trustee of the Trust for Public Land, where he served as national chairman for seven years; as a director of the Rocky Mountain Institute; as a director of BeltLine Partnership, Inc.; as chairman of the Capital Campaign for the Chattahoochee Nature Center; as president of the West Hill Foundation for Nature; and as chairman of the Yale Divinity School Board of Advisors. Sawyer previously served on the boards of IDI and EDAW as well as a trustee of the Urban Land Institute from 2002 to 2008.

Sawyer graduated from the University of North Carolina at Chapel Hill with a BA in English; was awarded a Rockefeller Fellowship and attended Yale Divinity School, from which he received his MDiv in 1975 and earned his JD from Duke University School of Law in 1978.

Rebecca R. Zimmermann
Denver, Colorado

Becky Zimmermann is a partner and the president of Design Workshop, an international land planning, urban design, and strategic services firm. She is highly recognized for her work with resort communities, including development strategy, market definition, positioning, and tourism planning; and in urban areas for brownfield redevelopment, development entitlements, and real estate economics. She is a frequent keynote speaker for a variety of conferences, including the Union of British Columbia Municipalities Conference on Sustainability, the ULI Recreation Development Council, and ULI Real Estate School. Her work has been published in *Metropolis*, *Landscape Architecture*, and *Urban Land* magazines.

Zimmerman holds an MBA from the University of Colorado, Denver, as well as a bachelor of communications and a bachelor of business administration from Trinity University in San Antonio, Texas. She is a member of the Young Presidents Organization, serves on the Riverfront Park Community Foundation Board of Directors, and is on the board of trustees for the National Sports Center for the Disabled.

Europe and the Middle East Jury

Ian D. Hawksworth, Jury Chair
London, United Kingdom

Ian Hawksworth is the managing director of Capital & Counties and an executive director of Liberty International PLC. Liberty International is a leading FTSE-100 ranking U.K.-listed real estate investment trust with property investments of over £8.2 billion. Through its two principal subsidiaries, Capital & Counties and Capital Shopping Centres, the group focuses on premier property assets that have scarcity value and require active management and creativity.

Previously, Hawksworth worked in Asia for 14 years. Based in Hong Kong, he was an executive director of Hongkong Land with responsibilities in commercial property and development.

Hawksworth has a bachelor's of science degree in estate management and is a member of the Royal Institution of Chartered Surveyors. He is a trustee of the Urban Land Institute, participates in the Harvard Real Estate Academic Initiative, and is a member of the British Property Federation Policy Committee.

Patrick Albrand
Paris, France

Shortly after joining Hines in 1995, Patrick Albrand helped establish its French subsidiary. At Hines, he has been active in the development of two high-rise towers in the business district of La Défense (Hines France's first major projects), Havas headquarters in Suresnes, and other projects.

Before joining Hines, Albrand was the director in charge of development at Stim-Bouygues Real Estate in Paris (1989 to 1995), where he arranged joint ventures with outside developers and investors. From 1983 to 1987, he was a senior research associate at the Lawrence Berkeley Laboratory in Berkeley, California, where he participated in the creation of tools and computer programs to manage energy consumption in buildings. From 1980 to 1982, he was with the Ministry of the Interior of Morocco, where he directed and managed a local department of public works that planned, designed, and developed 2,500 multifamily units, a mosque, and a hospital.

Albrand received a master's of architecture degree from the École des Beaux-Arts in 1980 and a master's of real estate development degree from Columbia University in 1988.

Andrea Amadesi
Milan, Italy

Andrea Amadesi is the managing director of AEW Italy, a subsidiary of AEW Europe (Natixis group–Paris). Prior to joining AEW, he worked in investment banking in Paris and Milan, holding a variety of management positions and specializing in asset management and real estate investment. From 1989 to 1992, Amadesi was employed by Sotheby's as managing director of Italian operations. He was also the founder of the Milan Modern and Contemporary Art Fair.

Amadesi holds a degree in economics and commerce from the Bocconi University of Milan. He is a governor of the ULI Foundation and served as chairman of ULI Europe from 2002 to 2005.

Anne T. Kavanagh
London, United Kingdom

Anne Kavanagh joined Cambridge Place Investment LLP in 2006 as senior portfolio manager for real estate in Europe and as a member of its real estate investment and real estate asset review committees. Previously, she was an international director at Jones Lang LaSalle (JLL), where she led the team that advised JLL on the acquisition of its initial European portfolio.

Since 2000, Kavanagh has specialized in working with clients on cross-border transactions in Europe. She was an operating executive of JLL's European Capital Markets, which transacted over £15 billion per annum in the last five years. From 2003 to 2005, she served on the board of Asset Management & Accounting Services, Ltd., a firm that managed 10 million square meters (108 million sf) of real estate across all sectors.

From 1993 to 1999, Kavanagh led the London West End capital markets advisory team for Jones Lang Wootton (JLL's predecessor firm), which she joined in 1983. She holds a bachelor's of science degree with honors in urban estate management from Nottingham Trent University and is a member of the Royal Institution of Chartered Surveyors.

Lee A. Polisano
London, United Kingdom

Lee Polisano is an architect and the president of Kohn Pedersen Fox (KPF), a leading international architectural practice recognized for design excellence, and a founding partner of KPF's London studio. Under his direction, the firm's work addresses a number of primary issues, namely a response to context, an awareness of the civic obligation of buildings, respect for the environment, and the importance of technology and innovation. He has published widely and is frequently invited to address academic and professional symposia.

Polisano is responsible for many notable projects across Europe, including the Heron Tower, London's first built-to-suit multitenant office building; The Pinnacle, the tallest building in London's central business district; and urban planning and regeneration projects in Paris, Milan, and Amsterdam.

He holds degrees from LaSalle College in Philadelphia (BA) and Virginia Polytechnic Institute (MArch); he was honored by the latter as the first recipient of VPI's Outstanding Professional Accomplishment Award. A Fellow of the American Institute of Architects, a member of the Royal Institute of British Architects and the Architektenkammer Berlin, he is a former cochair of ULI Europe's Office and Mixed-Use Council.

Andreas Schiller
Bergisch Gladbach, Germany

Andreas Schiller is editor in chief of the real estate Internet platform CompEtencE Circle, the yearbook *Europe Real Estate,* and the trade journal *EXPO REAL Magazine*. Starting in 1993, he worked as a freelance journalist, specializing in real estate and urban development, before he joined the editorial team of *Immobilien Manager* in 1996, where he was editor-in-chief from 1997 until 2003. In 2003, he was honored with the Deutscher Preis für Immobilienjournalismus (German Award for Real Estate Journalism).

Schiller is a member of ULI Germany's Executive Committee, serving as vice chair for communications and membership, as well as on the jury of the ULI Germany Leadership Awards and on ULI's European Membership Committee.

He specializes in reporting on international trends and innovative developments. He has a strong interest in central and eastern European countries. He organizes and heads conferences, panels, and other events in the real estate industry, and he cooperates with such real estate–related events as Expo Real, MIPIM, and Real Vienna.

Asia Pacific Jury

Yasuhiko Watanabe, Jury Chair
Tokyo, Japan

Yasuhiko Watanabe is a senior adviser at Mitsubishi Estate Company (MEC), Ltd., one of the largest real estate companies in Japan. He currently provides direct counsel to MEC's entire commercial real estate business, which includes the development, leasing, and management of over 4 million square meters (43 million sf) of office and retail space throughout Japan. Since he joined the company in 2000, he has played an integral role in MEC's large-scale reform of Marunouchi, Tokyo's premier business district.

Prior to joining MEC, Watanabe spent 36 years with the Bank of Tokyo–Mitsubishi, Ltd., where he served as a managing director responsible for its entire international planning. Earlier, he covered Europe, the Middle East, and Africa as well as Kyoto and Nagoya as a general manager.

Watanabe holds a bachelor's degree in economics from Keio University and a master's degree from the Wharton School at the University of Pennsylvania. He served as council chair of ULI Japan until March 2008, as vice chairman of the Japan Facility Management Promotion Association, and as a director of the Japan Building Owners and Managers Association. He is a member of the board of overseers at Keio University Business School.

Ivana Benda
Shanghai, China

Ivana Benda is a partner and design director of Allied Architects International (AAI), Inc., a design firm of more than 60 professionals licensed in Europe, North America, and China, that focuses on the China market. AAI's senior management team has completed more than 250 projects in China.

Before joining AAI, she was a senior associate, principal, coordinator, and design director in many international firms, such as Toronto-based B+H Architects International. Benda has more than 30 years of experience in all fields of the architectural profession. Although her design approach and basic understanding derive from her European education and background, most of her significant professional experience has been gained in North America and in China, where she began working in 1991.

Benda is a graduate of the Czech University of Technology, from which she received a master's degree in architecture and where she recently finished her doctoral degree studies as well. She is a member of the Ontario Association of Architects and the Royal Architectural Institute of Canada. She is often invited to speak and exhibit her work at national and international conferences and conventions and in public media. She is an active promoter of practice-oriented architectural education and likes to share her experience with young professionals through workshops and lectures. She joined ULI to promote sustainable land development and architecture in Asia.

Nicholas Brooke
Hong Kong, China

Nicholas Brooke is the chairman of Professional Property Services Limited, a specialist real estate consultancy based in Hong Kong, providing a selected range of advisory services across the Asia Pacific region. Having spent the last 25 years based in the region, Brooke is a recognized authority and commentator on property-related and planning matters and has provided advice in these areas to several Asian governments as well as the U.S. State Department.

He is a past president of the Royal Institution of Chartered Surveyors and a former member of the Hong Kong Housing Authority and the Hong Kong Town Planning Board. Currently, Brooke is chairman of the Hong Kong Science and Technology Park Corporation and of the Hong Kong Coalition of Service Industries as well as a member of the Hong Kong Harbourfront Enhancement Committee.

Brooke is a nonexecutive director on the board of MAF Properties, one of the Middle East's leading shopping center developers; of Vinaland Vietnam Real Estate Fund, the first Vietnam property fund to be listed on the AIM board of the London Stock Exchange; of Shanghai Forte Land, one of the largest residential developers in mainland China; and of China Central Properties Limited, another AIM-listed mainland property development company.

Silas Chiow
Shanghai, China

Silas Chiow is the director of Skidmore, Owings & Merrill (SOM) China in Shanghai. He is responsible for spearheading SOM's business strategies within China and facilitating its architecture and planning projects throughout Asia.

Chiow began his career at SOM's New York office in 1987, where he discovered his passion for the New York high rise while working on such notable projects as 180 Allyn Street, 320 Park Avenue, and the Wall Street Financial Center. In 1992, he won first prize at the Yokohama International Urban Design Competition and was invited to work in Nikken Sekkei's Tokyo office, where he worked on major civic projects such as the Tokyo Government Center at Saitama, as well as commercial projects in Tokyo and Singapore.

In 1995, Chiow joined SOM's San Francisco office, where he was assigned the mission of providing leadership for the firm's China initiatives. In his 21-year career as an architect, urban planner, and project manager, he has gained experience and expertise in many development products, including hospitality, retail, mixed use, residential, convention centers, institutions, multifamily housing, and hotels.

Raj Menda
Bangalore, India

Raj Menda is the managing director of RMZ Corp, a leading commercial and residential real estate company in India. RMZ, founded in 2002 by Menda and his family, has developed more than 1.2 million square meters (13 million sf) of Class A office space in Bangalore, Hyderabad, Chennai, Kolkata, and Pune. Its first green building was the first office building in India to receive a LEED Platinum certification. At RMZ, Menda is responsible for sourcing funds, striking deals, and developing and managing office, residential, retail, and hospitality properties.

Menda earned a graduate degree in commerce and business management. He is the honorary secretary of the National Real Estate Developers Association, which is a constituent part of the Confederation of Real Estate Developers Association of India, vice president of the State of Karnataka Ownership Apartment Promoters Association, an active member of the Global Real Estate Institute and the Urban Land Institute, and a founding member of the Bangalore chapter of the Young Presidents' Organization.

The following 247 projects have received ULI Awards for Excellence. Each project name is followed by its location and its developer/owner.

1979
First year of award

The Galleria; Houston, Texas; Hines Interests Limited Partnership

1980

Charles Center; Baltimore, Maryland; Baltimore City Development Corporation

1981

WDW/Reedy Creek; Orlando, Florida; The Walt Disney Company

1982
Two awards given: large and small scale

Large Scale: Heritage Village; Southbury, Connecticut; Heritage Development Group, Inc. • **Small Scale:** Promontory Point; Newport Beach, California; The Irvine Company

1983

Large Scale: Eaton Centre; Toronto, Canada; Cadillac Fairview Limited

1984

Large Scale: Embarcadero Center; San Francisco, California; Embarcadero Center, Ltd. • **Small Scale:** Rainbow Centre; Niagara Falls, New York; The Cordish Company

1985
Introduction of product categories

New Community: Las Colinas; Irving, Texas; JPI Partners, Inc. • **Large-Scale Residential:** Museum Tower; New York, New York; The Charles H. Shaw Company • **Small-Scale Urban Mixed Use:** Sea Colony Condominiums; Santa Monica, California; Dominion Property Company • **Large-Scale Recreational:** Sea Pines Plantation; Hilton Head, South Carolina; Community Development Institute • **Small-Scale Urban Mixed Use:** Vista Montoya; Los Angeles, California; Pico Union Neighborhood Council/Community Redevelopment Agency

1986
Introduction of rehabilitation and special categories

Small-Scale Mixed Use: 2000 Pennsylvania Avenue; Washington, D.C.; George Washington University • **Small-Scale Rehabilitation:** Downtown Costa Mesa; Costa Mesa, California; PSB Realty Corporation • **Special:** Inner Harbor Shoreline; Baltimore, Maryland; Baltimore City Development Corporation • **Large-Scale Recreational:** Kaanapali Beach Resort; Kaanapali, Hawaii; Amfac/JMB Hawaii • **Large-Scale Residential:** The Landings on Skidaway Island; Savannah, Georgia; The Bramigar Organization, Inc. • **Small-Scale Industrial/Office Park:** The Purdue Frederick Company; Norwalk, Connecticut; The Purdue Frederick Company • **Large-Scale Recreational:** Water Tower Place; Chicago, Illinois; JMB Realty Corporation

1987

Large-Scale Industrial/Office Park: Bishop Ranch Business Park; San Ramon, California; Sunset Development Company • **Small-Scale Commercial/Retail:** Loews Ventana Canyon Resort; Tucson, Arizona; Estes Homebuilding • **Large-Scale Urban Mixed Use:** St. Louis Union Station; St. Louis, Missouri; The Rouse Company • **Small-Scale Residential:** Straw Hill; Manchester, New Hampshire; George Matarazzo and Mark Stebbins • **Rehabilitation:** The Willard Inter-Continental; Washington, D.C.; The Oliver Carr Company

1988

Large-Scale Urban Mixed Use: Copley Place; Boston, Massachusetts; Urban Investment & Development Company • **Special:** Downtown Women's Center; Los Angeles, California; The Ratkovich Company • **Large-Scale Commercial/Retail:** The Grand Avenue; Milwaukee, Wisconsin; Milwaukee Redevelopment Corporation • **Rehabilitation:** Northpoint; Chicago, Illinois; Amoco Neighborhood Development • **Small-Scale Residential:** Pickleweed Apartments; Mill Valley, California; BRIDGE Housing Corporation • **Large-Scale Residential:** Rector Place; New York, New York; Battery Park City Authority • **Small-Scale Office:** Wilshire Palisades; Santa Monica, California; Tooley & Company

1989
Introduction of Heritage Award

Small-Scale Urban Mixed Use: Charleston Place; Charleston, South Carolina; The Taubman Company, Inc., and Cordish Embry Associates (joint venture) • **Rehabilitation:** Commonwealth Development; Boston, Massachusetts; Corcoran Management • **Small-Scale Office:** Escondido City Hall; Escondido, California; City of Escondido • **Large-Scale Office:** Norwest Center; Minneapolis, Minnesota; Hines Interests • **Special:** Pratt-Willert Neighborhood; Buffalo, New York; City of Buffalo • **New Community:** Reston; Reston, Virginia; Mobil Land Development in Virginia • **Heritage Award:** Rockefeller Center; New York, New York; The Rockefeller Group • **Large-Scale Urban Mixed Use:** Rowes Wharf; Boston, Massachusetts; The Beacon Companies

1990

Small-Scale Commercial: The Boulders; Carefree, Arizona; Westcor Partners • **Large-Scale Industrial:** Carnegie Center; Princeton, New Jersey; Carnegie Center Associates • **Small-Scale Residential:** Columbia Place; San Diego, California; Odmark & Thelan • **Large-Scale Residential:** River Run; Boise, Idaho; O'Neill Enterprises, Inc. • **Special:** Tent City; Boston, Massachusetts; Tent City Corporation • **Rehabilitation:** Wayne County Building; Detroit, Michigan; Farbman Stein • **New Community:** Woodlake; Richmond, Virginia; East West Partners of Virginia

1991

Small-Scale Commercial/Retail: Del Mar Plaza; Del Mar, California; Del Mar Partnership • **Large-Scale Urban Mixed Use:** Fashion Centre at Pentagon City; Arlington, Virginia; Melvin Simon & Associates, and Rose Associates • **Small-Scale Urban Mixed Use:** Garibaldi Square; Chicago, Illinois; The Charles H. Shaw Company • **Large-Scale Residential:** Ghent Square; Norfolk, Virginia; Norfolk Redevelopment and Housing Authority • **Special:** Grand Central Partnership; New York, New York; Grand Central Partnership • **Small-Scale Office:** James R. Mills Building; San Diego, California; Starboard Development Corporation • **Rehabilitation:** Marina Village; Alameda, California; Vintage Properties • **Special:** Union Station; Washington, D.C.; Union Station Redevelopment Corporation

1992

Small-Scale Commercial/Retail: CocoWalk; Miami, Florida; Constructa U.S. • **Special:** The Coeur d'Alene Resort Golf Course; Coeur d'Alene, Idaho; Hagadone Hospitality • **Special:** The Delancey Street Foundation; San Francisco, California; The Delancey Street Foundation • **Public:** Harbor Point; Boston, Massachusetts; Corcoran Jennison Companies • **Large-Scale Mixed Use:** Market Square; Washington, D.C.; Trammell Crow • **New Community:** Planned Community of Mission Viejo; Mission Viejo, California; Mission Viejo Company • **Small-Scale Residential:** Summit Place; St. Paul, Minnesota; Robert Engstrom Companies • **Rehabilitation:** Tysons Corner Center; McLean, Virginia; The L&B Group

1993

Small-Scale Residential: Beverly Hills Senior Housing; Beverly Hills, California; Jewish Federation Council • **Special:** Charlestown Navy Yard; Charlestown, Massachusetts; Boston Redevelopment Authority • **Heritage Award:** The Country Club Plaza; Kansas City, Missouri; J.C. Nichols Company • **Large-Scale Residential:** The Cypress of Hilton Head Island; Hilton Head Island, South Carolina; The Melrose Company • **Small-Scale Rehabilitation:** Furness House; Baltimore, Maryland; The Cordish Company • **Large-Scale Recreational:** Kapalua; Kapalua, Maui, Hawaii; Kapalua Land Company, Ltd. • **Special:** Post Office Square Park and Garage; Boston, Massachusetts; Friends of Post Office Square, Inc. • **Rehabilitation:** Schlitz Park; Milwaukee, Wisconsin; The Brewery Works, Inc. • **Small-Scale Commercial/Retail:** The Somerset Collection; Troy, Michigan; Forbes/Cohen Properties and Frankel Associates

1994
Introduction of international category

International: Broadgate; London, United Kingdom; Stanhope Properties • **Small-Scale Residential:** Orchard Village; Chattanooga, Tennessee; Chattanooga Neighborhood Enterprise • **Public:** Oriole Park at Camden Yards; Baltimore, Maryland; Maryland Stadium Authority • **Special:** The Pennsylvania Avenue Plan; Washington, D.C.; Pennsylvania Avenue Development Corporation • **Large-Scale Rehabilitation:** Phipps Plaza; Atlanta, Georgia; Compass Retail, Inc. • **Heritage Award:** Sea Pines Plantation; Hilton Head Island, South Carolina; Charles Fraser • **Large-Scale Office:** Washington Mutual Tower; Seattle, Washington; Wright Runstad and Company • **Large-Scale Residential:** Woodbridge; Irvine, California; The Irvine Company • **Special:** The Woodlands; The Woodlands, Texas; The Woodlands Corporation

1995

Small-Scale Rehabilitation: 640 Memorial Drive; Cambridge, Massachusetts; Massachusetts Institute of Technology Real Estate • **Large-Scale Commercial/ Retail:** Broadway Plaza; Walnut Creek, California; Macerich Northwestern Associates and The Macerich Company • **Heritage Award:** Disneyland Park; Anaheim, California; The Walt Disney Company • **Large-Scale Industrial/ Office:** Irvine Spectrum; Orange County, California; The Irvine Company • **Small-Scale Recreational:** Little Nell Hotel and Aspen Mountain Base; Aspen, Colorado; Aspen Skiing Company • **Special:** Monterey Bay Aquarium; Monterey, California; The Monterey Bay Aquarium Foundation • **New Community:** Pelican Bay; Naples, Florida; WCI Communities LP • **Special:** Riverbank State Park; New York, New York; New York State Office of Parks, Recreation and Historic Preservation • **Small-Scale Residential:** Strathern Park Apartments; Sun Valley, California; Thomas Safran and Associates

1996

Large-Scale Residential: Avenel; Potomac, Maryland; Natelli Communities • **Public:** Bryant Park; New York, New York; Bryant Park Restoration Corporation • **Large-Scale Office:** Comerica Tower at Detroit Center; Detroit, Michigan; Hines Interests Limited Partnership • **Small-Scale Residential:** The Court Home Collection at Valencia NorthPark; Valencia, California; The Newhall Land and Farming Company, and RGC • **Small-Scale Commercial/Hotel:** The Forum Shops; Las Vegas, Nevada; Simon Property Group • **Small-Scale Mixed Use:** The Heritage on the Garden; Boston, Massachusetts; The Druker Company • **Large-Scale Recreational:** Kiawah Island; Kiawah Island, South Carolina; Kiawah Resort Associates LP • **Special:** The Scattered Site Program; Chicago, Illinois; The Habitat Company

1997

Heritage Award: The Arizona Biltmore Hotel and Resort; Phoenix, Arizona; Grossman Company Properties • **Rehabilitation:** Chelsea Piers; New York, New York; Chelsea Piers LP • **Large-Scale Recreational:** Desert Mountain; Scottsdale, Arizona; Desert Mountain Properties • **Rehabilitation:** Eagles Building Restoration; Seattle, Washington; A Contemporary Theater and Housing Resources Group (general partners) • **Small-Scale Residential:** Mercado Apartments; San Diego, California; City of San Diego Redevelopment Agency • **Large-Scale Commercial/Hotel:** Park Meadows; Park Meadows,

Colorado; TrizecHahn Centers • **Special:** Pennsylvania Convention Center; Philadelphia, Pennsylvania; Pennsylvania Convention Center Authority • **Special:** A Safe House for Kids and Moms; Irvine, California; Human Options • **Public:** Smyrna Town Center; Smyrna, Georgia; City of Smyrna, Knight-Davidson Companies (residential) and Thomas Enterprises (retail/offices) • **International:** Stockley Park at Heathrow; Uxbridge, Middlesex, United Kingdom; Stanhope Properties PLC

1998

Large-Scale Business Park: Alliance; Fort Worth, Texas; Hillwood Development Corporation • **Special:** American Visionary Art Museum; Baltimore, Maryland; Rebecca and LeRoy E. Hoffberger • **International:** Calakmul; Mexico City, Mexico; Francisco G. Coronado (owner) • **Small-Scale Residential:** Courthouse Hill; Arlington, Virginia; Eakin/Youngentob Associates Inc. • **Public:** Harold Washington Library Center; Chicago, Illinois; U.S. Equities Realty (developer) • **Special:** Richmond City Center; Richmond, California; BRIDGE Housing Corporation (owner) • **Rehabilitation:** Twenty-Eight State Street; Boston, Massachusetts; Equity Office Properties Trust • **Rehabilitation:** UtiliCorp United World Headquarters/New York Life Building; Kansas City, Missouri; The Zimmer Companies • **Small-Scale Recreational:** Village Center; Beaver Creek, Colorado; East West Partners

1999

Small-Scale Rehabilitation: Bayou Place; Houston, Texas; The Cordish Company • **Large-Scale Residential:** Bonita Bay; Bonita Springs, Florida; Bonita Bay Properties Inc. • **Public:** Chicago Public Schools Capital Improvement Program; Chicago, Illinois; Chicago Public Schools • **Small-Scale Commercial/Hotel:** The Commons at Calabasas; Calabasas, California; Caruso Affiliated Holdings • **Special:** Coors Field; Denver, Colorado; Denver Metropolitan Stadium District • **Small-Scale Mixed Use:** East Pointe; Milwaukee, Wisconsin; Milwaukee Redevelopment Corporation and Mandel Group Inc. • **Large-Scale Recreational:** Hualalai; Ka'upulehu-Kona, Hawaii; Ka'upulehu Makai Venture/Hualalai Development Company • **Large-Scale Rehabilitation:** John Hancock Center; Chicago, Illinois; U.S. Equities Realty • **Small-Scale Residential:** Normandie Village; Los Angeles, California; O.N.E. Company Inc. and SIPA (general partners) • **Small-Scale Commercial/Hotel:** Seventh & Collins Parking Facility (Ballet Valet); Miami Beach, Florida; City of Miami Beach, Goldman Properties • **International:** Vinohradský Pavilon; Prague, Czech Republic; Prague Investment, a.s.

2000

Small-Scale Rehabilitation: Amazon.com Building; Seattle, Washington; Wright Runstad and Company • **Heritage Award:** The Burnham Plan; Chicago, Illinois; The Commercial Club of Chicago • **Small-Scale Residential:** The Colony; Newport Beach, California; Irvine Apartment Communities • **Large-Scale Residential:** Coto de Caza; Orange County, California; Lennar Communities • **Small-Scale Mixed Use:** DePaul Center; Chicago, Illinois; DePaul University • **Public:** NorthLake Park Community School; Orlando, Florida; Lake Nona Land Company • **Large-Scale Rehabilitation:** The Power Plant; Baltimore, Maryland; The Cordish Company • **International:** Sony Center am Potsdamer Platz; Berlin, Germany; Tishman Speyer Properties, Sony Corporation, Kajima Corporation, and BE-ST Development GmbH & Co. (owner) • **Special:** Spring Island; Beaufort County, South Carolina; Chaffin/Light Associates • **Public:** The Townhomes on Capitol Hill; Washington, D.C.; Ellen Wilson CDC and Telesis Corporation • **Large-Scale Recreational:** Whistler Village/Blackcomb Benchlands; Whistler, British Columbia, Canada; Resort Municipality of Whistler, and INTRAWEST Corporation

2001
International category eliminated

New Community: Celebration; Celebration, Florida; The Celebration Company • **Special:** Dewees Island; Dewees Island, South Carolina; Island Preservation Partnership • **Large-Scale Residential:** Harbor Steps; Seattle, Washington; Harbor Properties Inc. • **Small-Scale Rehabilitation:** Pier 1; San Francisco, California; AMB Property Corporation • **Small-Scale Recreational:** The Reserve; Indian Wells, California; Lowe Enterprises Inc. • **Small-Scale Office:** Thames Court; London, United Kingdom; Markborough Properties Limited • **Special:** Townhomes at Oxon Creek; Washington, D.C.; William C. Smith & Company Inc. • **Large-Scale Mixed Use:** Valencia Town Center Drive; Valencia, California; The Newhall Land and Farming Company • **Large-Scale Commercial/Hotel:** The Venetian Casino Resort; Las Vegas, Nevada; LVS/Development Group • **Public:** Yerba Buena Gardens; San Francisco, California; Yerba Buena Alliance

2002

Small-Scale Mixed Use: Bethesda Row; Bethesda, Maryland; Federal Realty Investment Trust • **Large-Scale Mixed Use:** CityPlace; West Palm Beach, Florida; The Related Companies • **Special:** Envision Utah; Salt Lake City, Utah; Coalition for Utah's Future • **Public:** Homan Square Community Center Campus; Chicago, Illinois; Homan Square Community Center Foundation (owner) and The Shaw Company (developer) • **Small-Scale Rehabilitation:** Hotel Burnham at the Reliance Building; Chicago, Illinois; McCaffery Interests • **Special:** Memphis Ballpark District; Memphis, Tennessee; Memphis Redbirds Foundation (owner), and Parkway Properties Inc. (developer) • **Large-Scale Office:** One Raffles Link; Singapore Central, Singapore; Hongkong Land Property Co. Ltd. • **Small-Scale Rehabilitation:** REI Denver Flagship Store; Denver, Colorado; Recreational Equipment Inc. • **Large-Scale Recreational:** Station Mont Tremblant; Quebec, Canada; Intrawest • **New Community:** Summerlin North; Las Vegas, Nevada; The Rouse Company

2003
Product categories eliminated

Atago Green Hills; Tokyo, Japan; Mori Building Company • Ayala Center Greenbelt 3; Makati City, Manila, Philippines; Ayala Land Inc. • Bay Harbor; Bay Harbor, Michigan; Victor International Corporation • Chattahoochee River Greenway; Georgia; Chattahoochee River Coordinating Committee • The Grove and Farmers Market; Los Angeles, California; Caruso Affiliated Holdings (The Grove), and A.F. Gilmore Company (Farmers Market) • Millennium Place; Boston, Massachusetts; Millennium Partners/MDA Associates • Shanghai Xintiandi (North Block); Shanghai, China; Shui On Group • The Town of Seaside; Seaside, Florida; Seaside Community Development Corporation • The Villages of East Lake; Atlanta, Georgia; East Lake Community Foundation Inc. • The West Philadelphia Initiatives; Philadelphia, Pennsylvania; University of Pennsylvania

2004 The Americas and Asia Pacific:

Baldwin Park; Orlando, Florida; Baldwin Park Development Company • Fall Creek Place; Indianapolis, Indiana; City of Indiana (owner), Mansur Real Estate Services Inc., and King Park Area Development Corporation (developers) • First Ward Place/The Garden District; Charlotte, North Carolina; City of Charlotte (owner), Banc of America Community Development Corporation (master developer) • The Fullerton Square Project; Singapore; Far East Organization/ Sino Land • Playhouse Square Center; Cleveland, Ohio; Playhouse Square Foundation • The Plaza at PPL Center; Allentown, Pennsylvania; Liberty

Property Trust • Technology Square at Georgia Institute of Technology; Atlanta, Georgia; Georgia Institute of Technology and Georgia Tech Foundation (owners), Jones Lang LaSalle (development manager) • University Park at MIT; Cambridge, Massachusetts; Forest City Enterprises, City of Cambridge Community Development Department, and Massachusetts Institute of Technology • Walt Disney Concert Hall; Los Angeles, California; Los Angeles County (owner), Walt Disney Concert Hall Inc. (developer) • WaterColor; Seagrove Beach, Florida; The St. Joe Company

2004 Europe:
Introduction of separate European awards program

Brindleyplace; Birmingham, United Kingdom; Argent Group PLC • Bullring; Birmingham, United Kingdom; The Birmingham Alliance • Casa de les Punxes; Barcelona, Spain; Inmobiliaria Colonial • Diagonal Mar; Barcelona, Spain; Hines Interests España • Promenaden Hauptbahnhof Leipzig; Leipzig, Germany; ECE Projektmanagement GmbH & Co., Deutsche Bahn AG, and DB Immobilienfonds • Regenboogpark; Tilburg, The Netherlands; AM Wonen

2005 The Americas:
34th Street Streetscape Program; New York, New York; 34th Street Partnership • 731 Lexington Avenue/One Beacon Court; New York, New York; Vornado Realty Trust • **Heritage Award:** The Chautauqua Institution; Chautauqua, New York; The Chautauqua Institution • Fourth Street Live!; Louisville, Kentucky; The Cordish Company • The Glen; Glenview, Illinois; The Village of Glenview and Mesirow Stein Real Estate Inc. • Harbor Town; Memphis, Tennessee; Henry Turley Company and Belz Enterprises • The Market Common, Clarendon; Arlington, Virginia; McCaffery Interests Inc. • Millennium Park; Chicago, Illinois; City of Chicago and Millennium Park Inc. • Pueblo del Sol; Los Angeles, California; The Related Companies of California, McCormack Baron Salazar, The Lee Group, and Housing Authority of the City of Los Angeles • Time Warner Center; New York, New York; The Related Companies LP • Ville Plácido Domingo; Acapulco, Mexico; Casas Geo and CIDECO-Anáhuac

2005 Europe:
Cézanne Saint-Honoré; Paris, France; Société Foncière Lyonnaise and Predica • Danube House; Prague, Czech Republic; Europolis Real Estate Asset • Government Offices Great George Street; London, United Kingdom; Stanhope PLC and Bovis Lend Lease • De Hoftoren; The Hague, The Netherlands; ING Real Estate Development • Meander; Amsterdam, The Netherlands; Het Oosten Kristal and Latei

2005 Asia Pacific:
Introduction of separate Asia Pacific awards program

Federation Square; Melbourne, Australia; Federation Square Management • Hangzhou Waterfront; Hangzhou, China; Hangzhou Hubin Commerce & Tourism Company Ltd. • The Loft; Singapore; CapitaLand Residential Ltd. • Marunouchi Building; Tokyo, Japan; Mitsubishi Estate Company Ltd. • Pier 6/7, Walsh Bay; Sydney, Australia; Mirvac Group and Transfield Holdings Pty Ltd.

2006 The Americas:
Belmar; Lakewood, Colorado; Continuum Partners LLC, McStain neighborhoods, and Trammell Crow Residential • Ladera Ranch; Orange County, California; Rancho Mission Viejo and DMB Consolidated Holdings LLC • Los Angeles Unified School District Construction Program; Los Angeles, California; Los Angeles Unified School District • Mesa Arts Center; Mesa, Arizona; Mesa Arts Center • Montage Resort and Spa; Laguna Beach,

California; The Athens Group • Prudential Center Redevelopment; Boston, Massachusetts; Boston Properties Inc. • Stapleton District 1; Denver, Colorado; Forest City Enterprises • The Presidio Trust Management Plan; San Francisco, California; The Presidio Trust • Victoria Gardens; Rancho Cucamonga, California; Forest City Commercial Development and Lewis Group of Companies • Washington Convention Center; Washington, District of Columbia; Washington Convention Center Authority

2006 Europe:
Agbar Tower; Barcelona, Spain; Layetana Developments • Muziekgebouw aan 't IJ; Amsterdam, The Netherlands; Dienst Maatschappelikjke Ontwikkeling • New Milan Fair Complex; Milan, Italy; Fondazione Fiera Milan • Potsdamer Platz Arkaden; Berlin, Germany; ECE Projektmanagement GmbH • Tour CBX; Paris la Défense, France; Tishman Speyer

2006 Asia Pacific:
Glentrees; Singapore; CapitaLand Residential Singapore • Izumi Garden; Tokyo, Japan; Sumitomo Realty and Development Company Ltd. • Luohu Land Port and Train Station; Shenzhen, China; Shenzhen Municipal Planning Bureau • Singapore Conservation Programme; Singapore; Singapore Urban Redevelopment Authority • Wuxi Li Lake Parklands; Wuxi, China; Wuxi Lake District Planning & Construction Leading Team Office

2007 The Americas:
1180 Peachtree; Atlanta, Georgia; Hines • 2200; Seattle, Washington; Vulcan Inc. • Daniel Island; Charleston, South Carolina; The Daniel Island Company • The Gerding Theater at the Armory; Portland, Oregon; Portland Center Stage • High Point; Seattle, Washington; Seattle Housing Authority • Highlands' Garden Village; Denver, Colorado; Perry Rose LLC and Jonathan Rose Companies • **Heritage Award:** King's Lynne; Lynn, Massachusetts; King's Lynne Residents Council and Corcoran Mullins Jennison Inc. • RAND Corporation Headquarters; Santa Monica, California; The RAND Corporation • San Diego Ballpark Neighborhood Revitalization; San Diego, California; San Diego Padres, JMI Realty Inc., Bosa Development, Cisterra Partners LLC, and Douglas Wilson Companies • THE ARC; Washington, D.C.; Building Bridges Across the River • Urban Outfitters Corporate Campus; Philadelphia, Pennsylvania; Urban Outfitters Inc. (owner) Philadelphia Industrial Development Corporation (developer)

2007 Europe and the Middle East:
Manufaktura; Łódź, Poland; Group Apsys • Meudon Campus; Meudon sur Seine, France; HinesFrance • Kanyon; Istanbul, Turkey; Eczacibasi Holding • Petit Palau; Barcelona, Spain; Fundació Orfeó Català-Palau de la Música Catalana • Terminal 4 at Madrid Barajas Airport; Madrid-Barajas, Spain; AENA (Aeropuertos Españoles y Navegación Aérea)

2007 Asia Pacific:
The Ecovillage at Currumbin; Currumbin, Queensland, Australia; Landmatters Currumbin Valley Property Ltd. • Hong Kong Wetland Park; Hong Kong, China; Architectural Services Department • The Landmark Scheme; Hong Kong, China; Hongkong Land • Nihonbashi Mitsui Tower; Tokyo, Japan; Mitsui Fudosan Co. Ltd. • Roppongi Hills; Tokyo, Japan; Mori Building Co. Ltd.

Project names in red indicate ULI Heritage Award winners.

Project names in blue indicate ULI Global Award for Excellence winners.

The ULI Global Awards for Excellence recognize projects that provide the best cross-regional lessons in land use practices. Up to five global winners may be named each year—chosen from among the year's 20 winners in the Americas, Europe, and Asia Pacific—by a select jury of international members.

In 2007, there were five global winners, which were announced October 26 at the ULI Fall Meeting in Las Vegas. On October 30, 2008, up to five Global Award winners will be announced at the Fall Meeting in Miami Beach.

Because the Global Awards jury considers only projects that have been judged to have met ULI's criteria for an Award for Excellence, the jury bases its award determination on how projects meet the following additional standards:

- Establishing innovative concepts or standards for development that can be emulated around the world;
- Showing strong urban design qualities;
- Responding to the context of the surrounding environment;
- Exemplifying, where applicable, universally desirable principles of development, such as sustainability, environmental responsibility, pedestrian-friendly design, smart growth practices, and development around transit; and
- Demonstrating relevance to the present and future needs of the community in which they are located.

Winners of the 2007 Global Awards for Excellence

High Point
Seattle, Washington
Owner/Developer: Seattle Housing Authority

Jury Statement: Solutions to two pressing needs in Seattle's housing market—environmental sustainability and the inclusion of affordable housing within mixed-income communities—converge at High Point. The public sector developer has created a healthy and sustainable environment for the High Point neighborhood and at buildout will have replaced 716 units of post–World War II public housing with 1,600 new units, almost half of which are designated affordable or for low-income tenants.

Hong Kong Wetland Park
Hong Kong, China
Owner/Developer: Architectural Services Department, Hong Kong Special Administrative Region Government

Jury Statement: Having started out as a prosaic wetlands conservation initiative, the Hong Kong Wetland Park blossomed in its planning stage into an educational facility to demonstrate best practices in environmental reclamation and sustainability and also into a tourist attraction. The park has succeeded on all counts, demonstrating a sound investment of public funds.

Manufaktura

Łódź, Poland

Owner/Developer: Group Apsys

Jury Statement: Manufaktura selectively preserves an abandoned industrial complex and resurrects it as a lifestyle destination center in Poland's second-largest city. The high-risk venture has catalyzed regeneration in Łódź, where its fresh interpretation of a *rynek*—a traditional Polish market square—has attracted new cultural, entertainment, and conference facilities.

Meudon Campus

Mudeon sur Seine, France

Owner: Vendome Croidor (Groupe AXA)
Developer: Hines France

Jury Statement: Meudon Campus returns a brownfield site not only to usability but also to environmental sustainability. Located on the Seine halfway between two burgeoning Paris submarkets for commercial properties, this five-building office park with green roofs and other environment-friendly features offers an alternative to more densely developed commercial centers nearby.

Urban Outfitters Corporate Campus

Philadelphia, Pennsylvania

Owner: Urban Outfitters Inc.
Developer: Philadelphia Industrial Development Corporation

Jury Statement: By seizing on an opportunity to move from its downtown Philadelphia headquarters to the newly decommissioned Philadelphia Navy Yard, the national retailing brand lived up to the image of its merchandising and marketing—edgy and urban. The company's sustainable redevelopment of former industrial buildings for use as a corporate headquarters fits seamlessly with its image and goals.

PHOTOGRAPHS BY DOUG J. SCOTT (210T); DANIEL WONG (210B); APSYS (211T); HERVÉ ABBADIE (211M); LARA SWIMMER (211B)

Legend: P = primary use (blue), S = secondary use (red)

Page	Project Name	Location	Project Area	Office	Residential	Retail	Entertainment/Restaurant	Hotel	Industrial	Civic	Medical/Education	Parks/Open Space
Americas			**(in acres)**									
2	Adidas Village	Portland, Oregon, USA	11.0	P								P
66	Atelier|505	Boston, Massachusetts, USA	1.2		P	S	P				S	
102	Avalon Chrystie Place/Bowery Place	New York, New York, USA	3.2		P	S	P			P		S
132	Army Residential Communities Initiative	USA	n/a	S	P	S				S		P
162	Carneros Inn	Napa, California, USA	27.0		P	S		P				
196	Chaparral Water Treatment Facility	Scottsdale, Arizona, USA	29.0	S					P	P	S	P
106	Church Street Plaza	Evanston, Illinois, USA	7.2	P	P	P	P	P				
78	Clipper Mill	Baltimore, Maryland, USA	17.5	P	P	S						P
138	Eleven80	Newark, New Jersey, USA	0.3		P	S						
84	General Motors Renaissance Center	Detroit, Michigan, USA	152.0	P	S	P	P	P	P	S	S	S
114	Liberty Hotel/Yawkey Center	Boston, Massachusetts, USA	3.0				S	P			P	
122	Lincoln Square	Bellevue, Washington, USA	32.1	P	P	P	P	P				
20	Medinah Temple–Tree Studios	Chicago, Illinois, USA	0.7	P		P						
90	National Ballet School of Canada/Radio City	Toronto, Ontario, Canada	2.4		P	S	S				P	S
174	New Columbia	Portland, Oregon, USA	82.0	S	P	S	S			P	S	P
190	Overture Center	Madison, Wisconsin, USA	2.5	S	P	S	P			P	S	
150	Solara	Poway, California, USA	2.5		P							S
126	South Campus Gateway	Columbus, Ohio, USA	7.5	P	P	P	P					
Europe and the Middle East			**(in hectares)**									
44	ADIA Headquarters	Abu Dhabi, United Arab Emirates	8.7	P		S	S					
166	Chimney Pot Park	Salford, United Kingdom	3.2		P							
110	Corvinus University	Budapest, Hungary	0.7	P		S	S				P	S
52	Hotel Wasserturm	Hamburg, Germany	0.6				S	P				
14	Kraanspoor	Amsterdam, The Netherlands	1.3	P								
26	Meydan Shopping Square	Istanbul, Turkey	13.0			P	S					S
56	Pall Italia	Buccinasco, Italy	8.8	P					P			
32	Stadsfeestzaal	Antwerp, Belgium	0.8		S	P						
38	Unilever House	London, United Kingdom	0.4	P								
156	Val d'Europe Downtown District	Marne la Vallée, France	150.0	S	P	P	P			S	S	S
60	Złote Tarasy	Warsaw, Poland	3.2	P		P	S					S
Asia Pacific			**(in hectares)**									
72	Beijing Finance Street	Beijing, China	31.0	P	P	P	S	P		S		S
184	Bras Basah.Bugis	Singapore	95.0	P	P	P	S	P		P	P	S
8	Elements at Kowloon Station	Hong Kong, China	13.5			P	S					S
170	The Fifth Garden	Shenzhen, China	11.2		P	S	S					S
48	Gateway Mall	Quezon City, Philippines	1.6	P		P	S					
144	Kirinda Project	Kirinda, Sri Lanka	1.2		P							
118	Life Hub @ Daning	Shanghai, China	5.5	P		P	S				S	P
178	Savannah CondoPark	Singapore	5.5		P							
96	Tokyo Midtown	Tokyo, Japan	6.9	P	P	P	S	P		S	P	S

■ indicates primary use   ■ indicates secondary use